# What's Your Agatha Christie I.Q.?

## 1,001 Puzzling Questions About the World's Most Beloved Mystery Writer

### Kathleen Kaska

A Citadel Press Book
Published by Carol Publishing Group

This book is dedicated to Lito;
with special thanks to
Jenny, Jane, Peg, Patty, Linda, my family, and, of course,
Lloyd—my very own Hercule Poirot.

Copyright © 1996 Kathleen Kaska
All rights reserved. No part of this book may be reproduced in any form,
except by a newspaper or magazine reviewer who wishes to quote brief
passages in connection with a review.

A Citadel Press Book
Published by Carol Publishing Group
Citadel Press is a registered trademark of Carol Communications, Inc.

Editorial, sales and distribution, rights and permissions inquiries should be
addressed to Carol Publishing Group, 120 Enterprise Avenue, Secaucus, N.J.
07094

In Canada: Canadian Manda Group, One Atlantic Avenue, Suite 105,
Toronto, Ontario M6K 3E7

Carol Publishing Group books may be purchased in bulk at special discounts
for sales promotion, fund-raising, or educational purposes. Special editions
can be created to specifications. For details, contact Special Sales
Department, 120 Enterprise Avenue, Secaucus, N.J. 07094.

Manufactured in the United States of America
10  9  8  7  6  5  4  3  2  1

Library of Congress Cataloging-in-Publication Data

Kaska, Kathleen.
    What's your Agatha Christie I.Q.? : 1,001 puzzling questions about
the world's most beloved mystery writer / Kathleen Kaska.
        p.  cm.
    "A Citadel Press book."
    1. Christie, Agatha, 1890–1976—Miscellanea.    2. Detective and
mystery stories, English—Miscellanea.    3. Women and literature—
England—Miscellanea.    4. Questions and answers.    I. Title.
PR6005.H66Z7   1996
823'.912—dc20                                                    96-31083
                                                                        CIP

# What's Your Agatha Christie I.Q.?

# Contents

# Part I

# Questions

# 1

# Agatha's Mysteries

Stabbed in the back in the train station during rush hour—no witnesses. Strangled in a phone booth during lunch time—impossible. Stabbed in the heart during a quiet bridge game—everyone has an alibi. Murder, the ultimate crime—lurid and shocking, but a perfect setting for a game between the author and reader. Writing a mystery involves more than merely telling a story. It requires a special skill and perhaps a sharp, twisted mind. The plot tenders a challenge full of intricate puzzles, hidden motives, and red herrings. All the evidence is laid out. All the suspects are revealed. It's time for the reader to unweave the tangled drama and unmask the murderer.

Chapter one includes ten quizzes regarding titles and plots, crimes and motives, aliases, murder weapons, settings, and much more. Good luck with your investigation!

## Quiz I: Titles and Plots

Quiz one contains short synopses of thirty Agatha Christie mysteries. Read the descriptions and identify the books.

1. Nick Buckley apparently had nine lives and was using them up rather quickly. Six unsuccessful attempts were made on her life. Hercule Poirot was outsmarted by her assassin. However, Poirot used his "little gray cells" along with the help of Scotland Yard to ferret out the criminal among all the possible suspects.

2. An archaeological dig in Iraq was the setting for a murder. The victim predicted her own death. The local authorities in Baghdad were stumped, but they were in luck. Hercule Poirot was passing through and was easily persuaded to help. Nurse Latheran became his assistant, but before they solved the case another apparent murder was committed.

3. Mistaken identities, dangerous blondes, manicured nails, and the sash of a dress were clues that Miss Jane Marple used to solve a murder that stumped Superintendent Harper and his assistants.

4. Suspects in the murder of Arlena Stuart Marshall included Captain Marshall, Patrick and Christine Redfern, a minister, a dress designer, and an offensive Englishman. While on vacation at a seaside resort, Hercule Poirot unraveled the mystery.

5. A conversation overhead at a bus stop allowed Hercule Poirot to discover the truth surrounding the unusual deaths of a baron who was stabbed in the neck and an actress who fell victim to an overdose of Veronal.

6. Amateur detective Luke Fitzwilliam investigated several mysterious deaths in the small village of Wychwood-under-Ashe. Finding too many motives and suspects, Mr. Fitzwilliam called in Scotland Yard to help solve this case.

7. After an Easter gathering with her greedy relatives, a wealthy spinster changed her will and left her entire estate to a female companion. Shortly thereafter the dowager died, but not before mailing a frightened letter to Hercule Poirot.

8. Midge loved Edward, who loved Henrietta, who loved John, who loved Veronica, who was not his wife. Jealousy and rejection led to a tangled murder sorted out by none other than our favorite Belgian, Hercule Poirot.

9. After warning his half-sister Loraine about a "secret society," Gerry Wade was mysteriously murdered. Superintendent Battle was called in to investigate while Lady Eileen "Bundle" Brent tried her hand at detective work.

10. A huge boulder fell from the top of Abu Simbel, Simon Doyle was shot in the leg, Linnet Doyle was shot in the head, Salome Otterbourne died from a gunshot wound, and a maid was stabbed to death. Hercule Poirot gathered the clues, analyzed the chain of events, and discovered the vengeful plot that led to murder.

11. Did the Nazis set forth a plan to invade England? Did Tommy and Tuppence Beresford stick their necks out a little too far this time? This mystery was a race against time.

12. Two people confessed to the same murder as Inspector Slack turned up eight other suspects. But the inspector's experience was no match for Miss Marple's knowledge of "human nature" as she politely suggested a plan to expose the real killer.

13. Yellow jasmine and a white bishop were two clues from the grave reckoned with by Poirot's "little gray cells."

14. Captain Hastings narrated the mystery that introduced Hercule Poirot. Both men settled in a small village in Essex. They subsequently became involved in the investigation of a murder by poisoning.

15. Murder was committed under the noses of four sleuths, Hercule Poirot, Mrs. Ariadne Oliver, Superintendent Battle, and Colonel Race. They finished their bridge game and turned to say good night, only to find that Mr. Shaitana was dead. He was stabbed in the chest while they trumped away.

16. Anonymous letters accusing residents and visitors in the town of Lymstock of immoral sexual liaisons led to murder. Miss Marple arrived on the scene, and you know the rest.

17. At the suggestion of a relative, Agatha Christie spiced up her murder stories. She wrote this thrilling and bloody mystery toward the end of 1938. It featured the meticulous Hercule Poirot trying to solve the murder of an arrogant, cruel millionaire.

18. This mystery was one of Dame Christie's favorites. A wealthy old man died: his insulin injection had been tampered with. Several family members, some driven

by greed and others by revenge, had motives, but they also had alibis. Chief Inspector Taverner, Assistant Commissioner Hayward, and an eleven-year-old girl investigated and discovered the truth.

19. A British agent's dying words, "Lucifer—Basrah—LaFarge," mystified those involved in the gathering of the "Great Powers."

20. In this mystery Hercule Poirot refused to protect the murder victim simply because the astute Belgian did not like the man's face. However, he agreed to track down the murderer as he and several suspects railed to their destination.

21. A healthy young man was mysteriously stricken with a disease and died. Six months later his father died in his sleep. Aunt Cora voiced her skepticism concerning the father's death. Shortly thereafter she was murdered in her bed, and her companion was poisoned. Hercule Poirot, with the assistance of Mr. Entwistle and Mr. Goldby, solved this mystery.

22. Miss Marple went to the aid of her distressed school chum. The woman was living in an old Gothic manor recently transformed into a school for delinquent boys. Lights went out and a murder was committed. Miss Marple untangled the web of evidence in a backward fashion and solved the mystery.

23. A game involving murder and a hunt for clues was staged for a charity fete. Things seemed a bit odd, so Mrs. Ariadne Oliver summoned Hercule Poirot to nose around. The game became a reality, and the two sleuths engaged in a real murder hunt.

24. Many critics claim that this was Agatha Christie's best mystery. The murderer of a prominent resident of King's Abbot was discovered and the murderer's identity was not only a surprise, it was also a sorrow to many who read this book.

25. In this mystery the master detective doubted his own abilities. A serial killer was one step ahead of Hercule Poirot in spite of the fact that the killer provided Poirot with important clues leading to the next victim.

26. A man brought his present wife and his ex-wife together at the annual family reunion. His mother was murdered. Was this a case of one daughter-in-law too many? Superintendent Battle fitted together the pieces of this intriguing puzzle.

27. Bobby Jones was on the seventeenth hole when his ball landed in a ravine. Upon fetching it, he stumbled upon an injured man just in time to hear his last words. A short time later, two attempts were made on Bobby's life. He solicited the help of a beautiful young "Lady," and with the aid of disguise, they managed to keep him alive and solve the mystery.

28. A bored young widow succumbed to the demands of a blackmailer even though he was extorting the wrong widow. Shortly afterward, the blackmailer was found dead in her library. A perfect stranger appeared just as the young widow discovered the body. She immediately trusted the stranger and allowed him to dispose of the body rather than call the police. The stage was set for this romantic murder mystery.

29. A nursery rhyme and little china figures accompanied one death after another. The potential victims were stranded on an island and there was no help in sight.

30. A case of amnesia led to the conviction of an innocent man. The amnesia victim recovered and remembered. The innocent man's family was not happy to have his name cleared. They would then become suspects for the murder. The amnesia victim responsible for the turn of events sought to alleviate his guilt and see that justice was served, no matter what.

## Quiz 2: Alternate Titles

Twenty-five of Agatha Christie's mysteries were published under alternate titles. This is a matching quiz that will require you to match the original title with the alternate title. Some have more than one.

1. *Murder at Hazelmoor*
2. *The Boomerang Clue*
3. *So Many Steps to Death*
4. *The Patriotic Murders*
5. *Poirot Loses a Client*
6. *Murder on the Orient Express*
7. *Funerals Are Fatal*
8. *Thirteen at Dinner*
9. *Easy to Kill*
10. *Murder in Three Acts*
11. *Murder in Retrospect*
12. *Murder for Christmas*
13. *Murder After Hours*

a. *Hickory, Dickory, Dock*
b. *Death in the Clouds*
c. *The Mirror Crack'd from Side to Side*
d. *Murder in the Mews*
e. *The Hollow*
f. *The Sittaford Mystery*
g. *Destination Unknown*
h. *Three Act Tragedy*
i. *Why Didn't They Ask Evans?*
j. *Taken at the Flood*
k. *Mystery at Littlegreen House*

14. *Hickory, Dickory, Death*
15. *Death in the Air*
16. *Ten Little Indians*
17. *Murder With Mirrors*
18. *Remembered Death*
19. *What Mrs. McGillicuddy Saw!*
20. *The Mirror Crack'd*
21. *Towards Zero*
22. *There Is a Tide*
23. *Mrs. McGinty's Dead*
24. *Dead Man's Mirror*
25. *Mr. Parker Pyne, Detective*

l. *4:50 From Paddington*
m. *And Then There Were None*
n. *Dumb Witness*
o. *An Overdose of Death*
p. *Blood Will Tell*
q. *Come and Be Hanged*
r. *After the Funeral*
s. *Parker Pyne Investigates*
t. *Murder She Said*
u. *Hercule Poirot's Christmas*
v. *Sparkling Cyanide*
w. *Five Little Pigs*
x. *One, Two, Buckle My Shoe*
y. *They Do It With Mirrors*
z. *Lord Edgware Dies*
aa. *Murder in the Calais Coach*
bb. *Murder Is Easy*
cc. *A Holiday for Murder*

## Quiz 3: Murderers, Motives, and Victims

Quiz three describes crimes from twenty popular Christie mysteries. See if you can name the murderer, the motive, or the victim.

1. In *Murder on the Orient Express*, the victim was killed in his sleep. His body was riddled with multiple knife wounds. Many felt he deserved to die lest his sins go unpunished. Name the victim.

2. The clumsy Mrs. Badcock talked too much at a cocktail party. She spilled her daiquiri and Marina Gregg, the gracious hostess, offered Mrs. Badcock her own untouched drink. The party came to a premature close minutes when later Mrs. Badcock dropped dead. What was the motive for this murder in *The Mirror Crack'd*?

3. Afraid his past would catch up with him, Sir Charles Cartwright went to great lengths to eliminate the one person who could have him committed. His only motive for killing two of his victims in *Murder in Three Acts* was to ward off suspicion. Name the victim who knew Cartwright's secret.

4. Organized crime, bigamy, and robbery lurked under the roof of Bertram's Hotel, and a killer could have had his/her pick of murder motives. Why did Lady Sedgwick's estranged daughter kill Michael Gorman, a doorman in *At Bertram's Hotel*?

5. Ruth Kettering was on her way to Nice to rendezvous with an old lover. She was carrying the famous Heart of Fire ruby, a gift from her father. Her estranged husband was traveling on the same train with his mistress, who urged him to blackmail his wife. Ruth was strangled en route, and the ruby was stolen. What was the true motive for Ruth's murder in *The Mystery of the Blue Train*? Was it robbery, or had her husband taken blackmail one step too far?

6. In *Death Comes as the End*, Yahmose killed his father's concubine. She had convinced the old man to cut Yahmose and his two brothers out of his will. Yahmose was successful in removing the obstacle that stood in

his way to fortune, but he killed four more times. Who were the other victims, and why was the first murder not enough to satisfy this Egyptian?

7. In *Appointment with Death*, Mrs. Boynton ruled over her family like a tyrant. Emotional abuse was her weapon. Every member of her family had a motive for her murder. But when the desert dust cleared, Hercule Poirot knew the truth. Who killed this heartless woman?

8. As a houseguest he left something to be desired. He was always the last to rise. This habit caused the kitchen staff to be unduly stressed. Hoping to break him of sleeping late, his friends arranged a practical joke, but even seven alarm clocks could not wake a dead man. Who was this victim in *The Seven Dials Mystery?*

9. *A Murder Is Announced* is the title of this mystery. It is also the beginning of a personal ad in the *Cleghorn Gazette*. What appeared to be a game turned out to be the real thing—murder. Three people were killed, including sweet, old Dora Bunner. Miss Marple cornered the murderer and tricked her into confessing. Who was this murderer and why did she kill three people in cold blood?

10. When Honoria Waynflete's family became destitute, Lord Easterfield bought the family home and gave Honoria employment there as his secretary. She repaid him by trying to get him hanged for murders he didn't commit. Did he deserve such treatment? Honoria thought so. What was her motive for vengeance in this 1939 mystery, *Easy to Kill?*

11. Dr. and Mrs. Christow were married for many years and loved one another dearly. Why then did gentle Gerda kill her husband in the mystery *Murder After Hours?*

12. Mary Gerrard was poisoned by Nurse Hopkins. From her bag of tricks the nurse pulled out enough morphia to kill several people, but Mary was her only target. What was the motive for this murder in the Hercule Poirot mystery *Sad Cypress?*

13. *A Caribbean Mystery* set Miss Marple in a tropical paradise easing her rheumatism. Just when things were becoming a trifle monotonous, Tim Kendal murdered Major Palgrave by tampering with his medication. The two men were total strangers. Why did Kendal want to get rid of this elderly, boastful traveler? What was his motive?

14. There were two murders in St. Mary Mead, and Miss Marple hated murder. In *The Body in the Library*, she set a trap and caught the killer. Who were the two victims?

15. Christian Gulbrandsen came to Stonygates with a message for Lewis Serrocold. Little did Mr. Gulbrandsen know that he also gave Mr. Serrocold an irresistible motive for murder. What was this motive in *Murder with Mirrors?*

16. Dr. Quimper and his wife had been separated for many years. Each had made a new life. Out of the blue, Dr. Quimper called for a reunion and a possible reconciliation. The meeting resulted in the good doctor strangling his wife. A simple divorce wouldn't

do? Lucy Eyelesbarrow aided Miss Marple in discovering Dr. Quimper's motive in *What Mrs. McGillicuddy Saw!* What was Dr. Quimper's motive for murder?

17. Meadowbank School for Girls provided its young ladies with the best education in England; however, the teachers did not fare as well. Three teachers had been murdered, and the publicity was beginning to destroy the school's reputation. In *Cat Among the Pigeons*, Hercule Poirot located Mrs. Upjohn, and she identified the murderer. What was the motive behind this triple murder?

18. Love and money were the motives for Madame Giselle's murder. There were several suspects, including Hercule Poirot. Who was the real killer in *Death in the Air*?

19. In *Hallowe'en Party*, Michael Garfield, a landscape artist, killed six people and tried to sacrifice his own daughter on Kilterbury Ring, an ancient site for ritual worship. Garfield had a masterful plan which was to be carried out on a secluded Greek island. What was Garfield's plan and why did it require the death of so many victims? Can you name these unfortunate people?

20. Mrs. Lancaster laced Mrs. Moody's cocoa with poison, and the atmosphere at the Sunny Ridge Nursing Home turned cloudy. Tommy and Tuppence Beresford visited Aunt Ada, and a chain of events led Tuppence on the murderer's trail. When Tuppence discovered that Mrs. Lancaster was a serial killer, the murderess came after our aging heroine with a knife. Who were Mrs. Lancaster's other innocent victims in *By the Pricking of My Thumbs*?

## Quiz 4: Aliases

Many of Agatha Christie's characters, including her detectives, are hidden behind aliases. Some of them have more than one alias. See if you can unmask the imposters in this twenty-question quiz.

1. *Taken in the Flood*—Enoch Adren came to town with information from the past. Before his true identity was discovered, he was murdered. Rosaleen Cloade, a confused and scared widow, was keeping a secret, but the secret did not involve her dead husband. Who were these two imposters?

2. *Sad Cypress*—Nurse Hopkins induced Mary Gerrard to make a will and then she murdered her for the inheritance. But Nurse Hopkins was not related to Mary, or was she? Who actually was Nurse Hopkins?

3. *N or M?*—An agent went undercover and took a room at the Sans Souci to try to locate the Nazi spies responsible for leaking valuable wartime information. To Tommy Beresford's surprise, Mrs. Blenkensop was also staying at the seaside resort. He thought she was back in London, but she was doing her own detecting, under another name, of course. Who was the flirtatious Mrs. Blenkensop?

4. *Murder in Mesopotamia*—Two imposters were digging for artifacts on the banks of the Tigris River. One was disguised as a French monk and called himself Father Lavigny. The other imposter called himself Dr. Leidner. Who were these two imposters?

5. *The Clocks*—Mr. Curry was murdered in the home of a blind woman. Hercule Poirot appeared briefly as a

consultant to Inspector Hardcastle. Poirot pointed the inspector in the right direction, the murder was solved, and Mr. Curry's true identity was revealed. Who was this mysterious Mr. Curry?

6. *Pocket Full of Rye*—Albert Evans charmed the innocent and gullible Gladys into taking a post with the Fortescue household. Once ensconced in her new position, she was at his beck and call. Albert Evans, of course, was not his real name. Who was this dastardly Romeo?

7. *Murder on the Orient Express*—He boarded the train under the name of Ratchett, but we know him as the notorious kidnapper of the Armstrong child. What was the true identity of this most hated villain?

8. *Elephants Can Remember*—Dorothea Preston-Grey wore a dead woman's clothes and wig and even masqueraded as the new wife of the dead woman's husband. This imposter did not live long to enjoy her new identity. Whom did Dorothea Preston-Grey impersonate?

9. *The Mystery of the Blue Train*—Ada Mason's trip to Nice was cut short when she disembarked from the train in Paris at the order of her employer. Her story seemed airtight, but there was a leak in her alibi, and her true identity was revealed. Who was this actress?

10. *Hickory, Dickory, Death*—Sharp-tongued Nigel Chapman was a boarder at 26 Hickory Road, where thievery and vandalism turned into murder. Hercule Poirot solved the murder and revealed Nigel's true identity. Who was Nigel Chapman?

11. *A Murder Is Announced*—Letitia Blacklock settled down to a quiet life in Chipping Cleghorn until a person from her past threatened to reveal her secret. She was successful in convincing old friends and acquaintances of her new identity, but this person from the past had information to prove she was not who she claimed. Who was Letitia Blacklock?

12. *So Many Steps to Death*—Hilary Craven took on the identity of a woman killed in a plane crash. She was on a mission with Agent Jessop to discover why scientists around the world were vanishing. Who was the woman Hilary Craven pretended to be?

13. *Murder in Retrospect*—Caroline Crale, named for her mother, used another name when she lived in Canada. What was Caroline's alias?

14. *Remembered Death*—Victor Drake wanted money badly enough to kill three people. Once these victims were out of the way, an inheritance would come directly to his mother. He had always been able to do what he liked with his mother. Drake's plan was foiled when Colonel Race recognized him. Under what name did the man known as Victor Drake serve time in prison?

15. *The Secret Adversary*—Sir James Peel Edgerton led two lives. He lived on both sides of the law. As Sir James, he was a well-respected criminal attorney, but he was also a criminal mastermind. What was the alias he used in his life of crime?

16. *Third Girl*—Andrew and Mary Restarick committed murder in order to inherit an enormous fortune. Something about Mr. Restarick's past did not sit right

with Hercule Poirot. Upon solving the murder, Poirot disclosed the true identity of this notorious couple. What were their real names?

17. *Dead Man's Folly*—Sir George Stubbs couldn't inherit because his family had lost its fortune. A new identity and a dead wife would allow him to recuperate his losses. What was Sir George Stubbs's real name?

18. *Murder on the Links*—Hercule Poirot received an urgent message from Paul Renauld pleading for the "detective extraordinaire" to come to his assistance. Upon Poirot's arrival, he learned that Mr. Renauld had been murdered that morning. Hercule Poirot discovered the name of the murderer and he also discovered the true identity of Paul Renauld. What was Paul Renauld's real name?

19. *A Holiday for Murder*—Stephen Farr claimed to be Ebenezer Farr's son, and Pilar Estravados claimed to be Simeon Lee's granddaughter. Poirot unmasked their true identities and absolved them from murder. What were their real names, and who was Stephen's real father?

20. *The Patriotic Murders*—This actress had a repertoire that included many characters, two of whom were Mrs. Albert Chapman and Helen Montressor. Who was this master of deception?

## Quiz 5: Murder Settings

Quiz six describes twenty murder settings. Provide the title of the Agatha Christie mystery that correlates with the location described.

1. An old hotel in the heart of the West End of London made it through the blitz and urban renewal unscathed, but upon closer examination, it was revealed that this Edwardian-style hotel underwent some subtle, sinister changes.

2. A murder took place in Petra, capital city of the ancient Nabataeans. The body was found near an archeological dig site called the Place of Sacrifice.

3. There was a mysterious old home once known as "The Towers," in the small town of Kingston Bishop. It was now called Gipsy's Acre, and the locals believed it was cursed.

4. This mystery began in the Atlantic Ocean as the *Lusitania* was sinking. A young American girl was given secret papers as she climbed into the lifeboat. She survived the shipwreck, but disappeared upon landing. The story resumed in London as two young adventurers eager for excitement found themselves hot on the trail of the secret papers and the missing girl.

5. Many people are afraid to visit the dentist, but Dr. Morley's patients had a different kind of fear. Two people had been murdered at his office at Number 58 Queen Charlotte Street.

6. The Jolly Roger Hotel on Smuggler's Island, a resort on the coast of England, was not so jolly after one of the guests was found strangled on the beach.

7. The Old Manor House in the village of Jocelyn St. Mary had a history of murder—and we know that history repeats itself.

8. Hercule Poirot was vacationing at the Hotel Majestic near the scenic village of St. Loo on the Cornish Riviera, where a tenacious murderer left only faint footprints for Poirot to follow.

9. Ariadne Oliver and Hercule Poirot were in Cornwall trying to solve the mystery surrounding two deaths that occurred twenty years before. The bodies of a husband and wife were found on a cliff at their family estate.

10. Tongues were wagging in Market Basing, a village an hour and a half from London. Miss Arundell died and her estate was for sale. Hercule Poirot and Captain Hastings had reason to be suspicious of the circumstances surrounding her death.

11. Hercule Poirot and Captain Hastings began their lifelong acquaintance at Styles Court of Essex, where they solved their first murder. The old estate could not seem to shake its reputation, and several decades later another murder was committed under its roof.

12. *Kilmorden Castle* is a cruise ship bound for Cape Town. Murder, robbery, and espionage proved to be the main agenda on this luxury liner.

13. The mystery began on the terrace of Crow's Nest, a seaside bungalow in Loomouth, Cornwall. Two men were murdered. Hercule Poirot assisted Satterthwaite and Egg in bringing the criminal to justice.

14. A serial killer struck the quiet little villages of Andover, Bexhill, Churston, and Doncaster. He had an unusual technique for selecting the scene of the crime.

15. The Gull's Point estate in Saltcreek could only be reached by boat. That left the murder suspects in high water.

16. Warmsley Vale, "a microscopic old-fashioned market town that degenerated into a village," seemed farther away from London than twenty-eight miles. But no place is safe from crime. A stranger came to town with damaging information that eventually led to his demise. Hercule Poirot investigated the murder.

17. At the request of Superintendent Spence, Hercule Poirot traveled to Broadhinny to investigate a murder. Poirot was forced to stay in the only guest house in town where the doors never stayed shut, pets had the run of the house, and the cook cut her finger and bled over the beans she was preparing for lunch.

18. Gossington Hall seemed like the perfect place to dispose of a body, but the killer could not fool the police. The investigators knew that the victim had been killed at another location and the body moved to Colonel Bantry's home. It seemed like an open and shut case until another body was found.

19. Alderberry Manor was the setting for a murder that occurred twenty years ago. The wife was convicted of killing her husband. Their daughter, convinced of her mother's innocence, hired Hercule Poirot to vindicate the accused.

20. Little Paddocks sounds too innocent to be the setting for three murders, but murder knows no bounds. Miss Marple led Detective Craddock to a most unlikely killer.

## Quiz 6: Murder Weapons and Victims

In this quiz, match the cause of death to the victim and the mystery in which the death occurred.

**Cause of Death**

1. Small dagger from Tunis
2. Strangled in sleep, victim's face disfigured
3. Green baize tube (used to keep drafts from blowing under the door)
.4. Kitchen skewer inserted at the base of the skull
5. Nicotine-laced glass of port
6. Burned in the firepalce
7. Thorn laced with poison
8. Hit-and-run
9. Cyanide-laced champagne
10. Morphia slipped into a double brandy
11. Taxene in the marmalade
12. Knocked on the noggin with a cosh
13. Drowned in a bucket of apples

**Mystery/Victim**

a. *The Pale Horse*/Father Gorman
b. *Easy to Kill*/Miss Mildred Fullerton
c. *The Big Four*/Mr. Paynter
d. *Murder at Hazelmoor*/Captain Trevelyan
e. *The Mystery of the Blue Train*/Ruth Kettering
f. *Hickory, Dickory, Death*/Mrs. Nicoletis
g. *Postern of Fate*/Mary Jordan
h. *The Moving Finger*/Agnes Woddell
i. *The Clocks*/Mr. Curry
j. *Remembered Death*/Rosemary Barton
k. *Murder in Three Acts*/Sir Bartholomew Strange
l. *Endless Night*/Ellie (Fenella) Rogers
m. *Death in the Air*/Madame Giselle
n. *Hallowe'en Party*/Joyce Reynolds
o. *Sleeping Murder*/Helen Halliday

14. Bashed in the head eight times with a hatchet
15. Stabbed in the back and buried in a shallow grave on the golf course
16. Strangled by her possessive brother
17. Stabbed in the heart with a silver fruit knife
18. Poisoned by a salad mixed with foxglove leaves
19. Cyanide capsules in hay fever medication
20. Eserine put in the insulin bottle

p. *The Murder of Roger Ackroyd*/Roger Ackroyd
q. *Crooked House*/Aristide Leonides
r. *A Pocket Full of Rye*/Rex Fortescue
s. *Murder on the Links*/Paul Renauld
t. *Funerals Are Fatal*/Cora Abernathie Lansquenet

## Quiz 7: Quotations

Who spoke the following words of wisdom, doom, or warning? Quiz seven consists of fifteen questions. Name the character and the book.

1. "All life is a jest, Imhotep—and it is death who laughs last. Do you not hear it at every feast? Eat, drink, and be merry, for tomorrow you die? Well, that is very true for us here—it is a question only of *whose* death will come tomorrow."

2. "...On the one side, the man with unlimited money; on the other side, the man with unlimited debts. There is no question as to who will come out on top."

3. "Evil is not something superhuman, it's something less than human. Your criminal is someone who wants to be important, but who will never be important, because he'll always be less than a man."

4. "You see, don't you, that she's got to be killed?"

5. "One of the wild ones. Oh, we've some of them in every generation. You can't blame them, you can't bring them into the community and make them live in law and order. They go their own way. If they're saints, they go and tend lepers or something, or get themselves martyred in jungles. If they're bad lots, they commit the atrocities that you don't like hearing about. And sometimes—they're just wild!..."

6. "Cover her face; mine eyes dazzle; she died young...."

7. "Of course if we were only in Chicago I could get him bumped off quite easily, but you don't seem to run to gunmen over here."

8. "I'll kill him before I give him up to you."

9. "Did her mother kill her father or was it the father who killed the mother?"

10. "Was it your poor child?"

11. "Mademoiselle, if you had studied the laws of Mendel you would know that two blue-eyed people are not likely to have a brown-eyed child...."

12. "Teacher, do you say yolk of eggs is white or yolk of eggs are white?" When the teacher replies that one says yolk of eggs is white and yolks of egg are white,

Tommy says, 'Well, I should say that yolk of egg is yellow!'"

13. "He began to tell lion stories. A man who has shot lions in large quantities has an unfair advantage over other men."

14. "'The young Siegfried,' she said, and sighed again."

15. "The window, Nurse, the window."

## Quiz 8: First Lines

The following are twenty first lines to Agatha Christie mysteries. Try to identify a title from its first sentence.

1. "'Books!' said Tuppence."

2. "It is difficult to know quite where to begin this story, but I have fixed my choice on a certain Wednesday at luncheon at the Vicarage."

3. "In the corner of the first-class smoking carriage, Mr. Justice Wargrave, lately retired from the bench, puffed at a cigar and ran an interested eye through the political news in the *Times*."

4. *"In my end is my beginning...."*

5. "Mrs. Van Rydock moved a little back from the mirror and sighed."

6. "The Espresso machine behind my shoulder hissed like an angry snake."

7. "In every club there is a club bore."

8. "Who is there who has not felt a sudden startled pang at reliving an old experience or feeling an old emotion?"

9. "It was five o'clock on a winter's morning in Syria."

10. "Bobby Jones teed up his ball, gave a short preliminary waggle, took the club back slowly, then brought it down and through with the rapidity of lightning."

11. "The man behind the desk moved a heavy glass paperweight four inches to the right."

12. "Old Lanscombe moved totteringly from room to room, pulling up the blinds."

13. "It was dusk when he came to the ferry."

14. "That amiable youth, Jimmy Thesiger, came racing down the big staircase at Chimneys two steps at a time."

15. "Iris Marle was thinking of her sister, Rosemary."

16. "The memory of the public is short."

17. "In the hall of the Tigris Palace Hotel in Baghdad a hospital nurse was finishing a letter."

18. "Gwenda Reed stood, shivering a little, on the quayside."

19. "Fasten your seat belts, please."

20. "Mrs. Oliver looked at herself in the glass.

## Quiz 9: Last Words

See if you can identify twenty Christie mysteries from their last line or lines.

1. "But I wish Hercule Poirot had never retired from work and come here to grow vegetable marrows."

2. "Last time I had my hands on you, you felt like a bird—struggling to escape. You'll never escape now."

3. "Our friend Colin has married that girl. If you ask me, he's mad. All the best.
Yours,
Richard Hardcastle"

4. "So, Hastings,—we went hunting once more, did we not? *Vive le sport.*"

5. "There are some things that one has to face quite alone."

6. "For, as Mr. Ferguson was saying at that minute in Luxor, it is not the past that matters but the future."

7. "Despard said cheerfully, 'Let's stab him, Rhoda, and see if his ghost can come back and find out who did it.'"

8. "If you knew what you looked like that night with the fluffy pink wool all around your head, standing there and saying you were Nemesis! I'll never forget it!"

9. "*Pour moi*, every time the central heating..."

10. "And if Albert welcomes us with a charred chicken, I'll kill him!"

11. " 'Woof,' said Bob in energetic assent."

12. "She quoted softly the last lines of the poem:
'She has a lovely face;
God in His mercy lend her grace,
The Lady of Shalott.'"

13. "'*Nineteen, twenty, my plate's empty*—' And went home."

14. "...We must do all we can to make up to them for having such a dull time in this war...."

15. " 'That,' I said, 'is Joanna's little joke.'"

16. "Lady Dittisham got in and the chauffeur wrapped the fur rug around her knees."

17. "And then, displacing both these emotions, there came a surge of triumph—the triumph some specialist might feel who has successfully reconstructed an extinct animal from a fragment of jawbone and a couple of teeth."

18. "And just where does my story begin? I must try and think...."

19. "He repeated to himself: 'A most unusual woman.'"

20. "I wasn't going to stand that from Suzanne. I sent her a reply of one word, economical and to the point: *Platycephalic!*"

## Quiz 10: Characters

Try to identify the character names and book titles that correspond with the following twenty character profiles given in quiz ten.

1. He first appeared in *A Caribbean Mystery* commanding Nemesis to "speak up." He died several years later in another mystery. In his will he left Miss Marple 20,000 pounds to "properly elucidate" a certain crime. Who was this pious benefactor and in which mystery did he reappear?

2. Hercule Poirot was quietly enjoying his breakfast when a hysterical young girl barged in claiming she "may have committed a murder." Poirot described her as "an Ophelia devoid of physical attraction." Who was this confused and bewildered young girl?

3. This beautiful, levelheaded sleuth made both her debut and swan song in the same book. Although this type of young, independent sleuth was almost unheard of in the '20s, her female adversaries have taken their place among the most popular detectives of our times. Who was this adventurous newspaper correspondent who solved two murders while racing through Africa?

4. This "almost friendless" man was wrongly charged with murder. Due to his passive nature he did nothing to proclaim his innocence. Hercule Poirot described him as a "poor stick" and not only saved his neck from the gallows, but also provided him with a fiancée. Who was this shy scapegoat?

5. He married his "lust to kill" and "strong sense of justice" by selecting the legal profession as a career. He eventually gained a seat on the bench, but power and authority did not satisfy his growing need to murder. He began to "collect victims," murderers who had escaped punishment. He then proceeded to carry out their executions. His confession was discovered in a bottle floating in the sea. Who was this criminal?

6. This character was described as "large and solid and noticeable...somehow very English." His motto was "no unpleasantness" and he was true to his word. Who was this Scotland Yard detective featured in several Agatha Christie mysteries?

7. She took a First in math at Oxford and was destined for a brilliant academic career, but the life of an educator held no appeal, and she happily entered the life of a domestic servant. After all, "she had a taste for people." Her reputation grew throughout England, and within a few years she could pick and choose her employers and work when she wished. Miss Marple, now eighty-nine and not as spry as she once was, requested that her young friend take a position at Rutherford Hall to take care of a broken family and to locate a dead body. Who was this trustworthy housekeeper?

8. "She had on a red shirt, a short green jacket and a brilliant blue beret, and despite a certain resemblance to an organ-grinder's monkey—she had long sorrowful, dark eyes and a puckered-up face—she was distinctly attractive." She was also determined to keep her childhood friend alive even if it meant faking a car accident and convulsing in the home of a murderer. Who was this spunky, fearless character?

9. In the Agatha Christie novel he was a geophysicist; in the movie he was a paleontologist. One evening while driving on the main Redmyn to Drymouth road, he picked up a hitchhiker at the exact time a murder was being committed. The next day this scientist left for Antarctica as part of the Hays Bentley Expedition. The hitchhiker was arrested and subsequently hanged for the murder while the person who could provide an alibi for him was studying continental drift on the other side of the globe. Several months later, back from the ice continent, the scientist was horrified when he realized he could have prevented an innocent man's death. Who was this methodical character who used the scientific method to discover the truth?

10. He made a shorter but memorable appearance in an early Hercule Poirot mystery. His was famous for his macabre dinner parties. There was one party in particular where he displayed his collection of successful murderers—those who got away with the crime. Who is this "Mephistophelean" character?

# 2

# The Top Ten

Can an author make the protagonist the murderer or have every suspect either guilty or innocent? The Grand Dame of mystery writing did. She played by her own rules and pulled out all the stops to stump her readers. The ten mysteries featured in this chapter have appeared numerous times on stage, screen, and television. They represent Agatha Christie's unique storytelling skills and extraordinary ability to construct the most puzzling plots and surprise endings.

This section contains ten quizzes featuring Agatha Christie's most popular mysteries. Each quiz features ten short questions in each of the categories of characters, clues, and circumstances. You'll easily find these books on any bookstore shelf. Go for it.

## Quiz 11: *Murder on the Orient Express*

### Characters

1. Who assisted Hercule Poirot in the murder investigation?

2. Who found the victim's body?

3. Which character wore false teeth?

4. Who smoked a pipe?

5. Who was the world famous tragic Shakespearean actress traveling on the Orient Express?

6. Who was the passenger who did not hide her connection with the Armstrong family when interrogated by Poirot?

7. Who was the first character whom Hercule Poirot discovered lying in the initial investigation?

8. With what famous character did MacQueen confuse Hercule Poirot?

9. Which murder suspect's father was the district attorney who handled the Armstrong case?

10. Whose grease-stained passport contained a vital clue for Poirot's investigation?

## Clues

1. At what time was Poirot awakened by a groan coming from Rachett's berth next door?

2. Where was the murder weapon found?

3. Where was the Wagon Lit's uniform, believed to be worn by the murderer, found?

4. Where was the scarlet kimono, worn by an unknown person seen near the scene of the crime, found?

5. What evidence proved that the murderer was still on the train?

6. How many wounds were inflicted on the victim?

7. Who owned the lace handkerchief found in the victim's compartment?

8. Why did the victim's watch point to 1:15?

9. What led Poirot to speculate that the victiim was attacked by more than one person?

10. What words did Poirot find on a charred fragment of paper in the victim's compartment?

## Circumstances

1. What was the number of Hercule Poirot's berth after he moved into the first-class cabin on the second night of the trip?

2. What was the name of the coach in which the murder occurred?

3. How much did Ratchett offer to pay Poirot for protection from Ratchett's enemies?

4. Why did Hercule Poirot refuse to protect Ratchett?

5. In what country was the train stranded?

6. Why was the train stranded?

7. Which real-life kidnapping case paralleled the Armstrong case?

8. Why did Hercule Poirot carry a pair of curling tongs?

9. Which game were the count and countess playing after dinner on the night of the murder?

10. Where did the train make its last scheduled stop?

## Quiz 12: *Ten Little Indians*

### Characters

1. Which character came to the island with an assumed name and an ulterior motive?

2. What morally suspicious character brought a Bible to the island?

3. Who were the first guests to arrive on the island?

4. Who bought the island for Mr. Owen and made all the arrangements for the guests?

5. What was the name of the Devonshire boatman who brought the group to the island?

6. What was the name of the lover who jilted Vera Claythorne and whose memory continued to haunt her long after they parted?

7. Who admitted to committing a murder?

8. What were the names of the two baffled officers from Scotland Yard who investigated the murders?

9. Which character was not afraid of the "big bad wolf" and often boasted of his prowess?

10. What was Justice Wargrave known as in his profession?

## Clues

1. What incriminating message did Owen leave for his guests?

2. Who was the first victim in the long series of murders?

3. Which character slept well the first night, unconcerned with becoming the next victim?

4. Who felt tranquil and resigned at the prospect of not being able to leave the island?

5. Which character had access to drugs?

6. Who brought a gun to the island?

7. Who searched the island for a possible lunatic responsible for the crimes?

8. What happened to the missing shower curtain?

9. What happened to Miss Brent's knitting wool?

10. How was it possible to predict the next method of murder?

## Circumstances

1. What was the name of the island and where was it located?

2. On what date did the doomed guests arrive?

3. What was the name of the mainland village?

4. How did the island receive its name?

5. What was the title of the gramophone record played on the first night the guests arrived?

6. Which employment agency recommended Vera Claythorne as secretary to Mrs. Owen?

7. What model car did Tony Marston drive?

8. How did Mr. Owen greet his guests?

9. What was the name of the fishing trawler that discovered the manuscript that held the pieces of the puzzle?

10. Who saw the distress signals coming from the island?

## Quiz 13: *The Murder of Roger Ackroyd*

### Characters

1. What cunning character helped Hercule Poirot investigate the crime?

2. Who engaged Hercule Poirot to take the case?

3. To which fictional characters did Dr. Sheppard compare himself and Poirot?

4. What motto did James Sheppard use to describe the character of his sister, Caroline?

5. What did Major Blunt do for a living?

6. Now that Mrs. Ferrars was free to marry Roger Ackroyd, why did the couple not proceed with the wedding?

7. Who was blackmailing Mrs. Ferrars?

8. To whom was Ursula Bourne secretly married?

9. Who left the silver table open in Roger Ackroyd's study?

10. Whom did Flora Ackroyd ultimately choose as her husband?

## Clues

1. Who stole the money from Ackroyd's desk the night of the murder?

2. Why was the grandfather chair moved away from the wall in the study where the body was found?

3. Which two clues did Hercule Poirot find after snooping around in the summerhouse?

4. What information did Mrs. Ackroyd withhold from her initial interview with Hercule Poirot?

5. What information did Mr. Raymond withhold from his initial interview with Hercule Poirot?

6. What did Hercule Poirot find in the goldfish pond behind Ackroyd's house?

7. What was Parker, the butler, hiding?

8. What was Miss Russell, the housekeeper, hiding?

9. What excuse did Poirot give for his trip to Cranchester?

10. Whose footprints were found on the window ledge leading from Roger Ackroyd's study?

## Circumstances

1. What was the name of Roger Ackroyd's house?

2. Which parlor game was popular among the characters?

3. What was the name of the village in which the murder occurred?

4. What was the name of the local inn where Ralph Paton stayed?

5. What was the name of Hercule Poirot's house?

6. What did Dr. Sheppard believe Hercule Poirot's profession was from his appearance and manner when they first met?

7. Where was Ralph Paton hiding during the investigation?

8. How long did Poirot give the murderer to do the right thing before Poirot went to the police with the incriminating evidence?

9. What was the color of the mysterious letter Roger Ackroyd received before he was murdered?

10. What was the name of the pub that Charles Kent used in his alibi?

## Quiz 14: *Crooked House*

### Characters

1. Who investigated Aristide Leonides's murder?

2. Who was Charles Hayward's father, and why was his advice so valuable?

3. How did Brenda earn her living before she married her wealthy husband, Aristide?

4. Why did Sophia have second thoughts about marrying Charles?

5. Who gave an accurate profile of the killer?

6. What was the name of the family attorney?

7. Who had possession of Leonides's new will, much to the dismay of his family and legal advisers?

8. Who was arrested for the murder of Aristide Leonides?

9. What did Clemency Leonides do for a living?

10. Which character outwardly expressed her joy and enthusiasm over Aristide's death?

**Clues**

1. What was eserine, the poison used to kill the victim?

2. In what kind of financial trouble was Roger Leonides?

3. To whom did Aristide Leonides leave his entire estate, and why?

4. Where were Brenda's love letters hidden?

5. Which character was the first to realize who the killer really was?

6. Where was Josephine's little black book hidden?

7. How were the dents on the washhouse floor made?

8. Why was there dirt on the seat of the old chair in the washhouse?

9. Why was Josephine's room ransacked?

10. Who suggested to the family an easy method for killing Aristide?

## Circumstances

1. What was the name of the restaurant where Charles and Sophia met when he returned from the war?

2. How did Aristide Leonides become so wealthy?

3. At what restaurant did Aristide and Brenda meet?

4. What type of work did Sophia do during the war?

5. Where did Roger and Clemency plan to set up their new home once they were free from Aristide's rule?

6. What was the name of the London suburb where the Leonides family resided?

7. Which Impressionist artist's work hung in the drawing room?

8. What was the name of the family catering business?

9. What was the name of the quarry in which the Ford was found?

10. What nursery rhyme was used to parallel the plot in this book?

## Quiz 15: *Death on the Nile*

### Characters

1. Whom was Linnet Ridgeway expected to marry before she announced her engagement to Simon Doyle?

2. Who joined the trip in Wadi Halfa and subsequently aided Hercule Poirot in the murder investigation?

3. Who did Ferguson turn out to be?

4. Whom did Ferguson want to marry?

5. Which two couples became engaged on the trip?

6. Why was Rosalie Otterbourne so protective of her mother?

7. From what mental illness did Miss Van Schuyler suffer?

8. Why was Jim Fanthorpe on the cruise?

9. Whom did Hercule Poirot compare to the Queen in *The Adventures of Alice in Wonderland*?

10. Who was behind the jewelry heist operation?

## Clues

1. Who taught Jackie de Bellefort how to shoot a pistol?

2. Where and how was the first attempt made on Linnet Doyle's life?

3. Poirot was a light sleeper. Why did he not hear the commotion at the time of the murder?

4. In whose stole was the murder weapon wrapped before it was disposed of?

5. What happened to Linnet Doyle's expensive pearls?

6. At what point in the story did Hercule Poirot realize the solution to the murders?

7. Why was Andrew Pennington on the trip?

8. What was the significance of the empty bottle of pink fingernail polish found in Linnet Doyle's cabin?

9. What was Dr. Bessner's motive that made him a suspect in Linnet's murder?

10. What motive made Miss Bowers a suspect in Linnet's murder?

## Circumstances

1. Which famous hotel did the guests stay at while in Assuan?

2. Which type of books did Salome Otterbourne write?

3. Which of her books did she recommend Poirot to read?

4. What was the title of Salome Otterbourne's latest book?

5. Which type of gun did Jackie de Bellefort own?

6. On which boat did Pennington say he left New York?

7. Which song was Jackie de Bellefort humming in the bar right before Simon Doyle was shot?

8. To which previous case from another Christie book did Hercule Poirot refer?

9. Which crime did Hercule Poirot hush up and not report to the police?

10. What did Hercule Poirot say was the main motive for most murders?

## Quiz 16: *The Murder at the Vicarage*

### Characters

1. Why was the vicar irritated by Inspector Slack's initial investigation?

2. What explanation did Miss Marple give for "viewing" the traffic on the lane about the time of the murder?

3. To what animal did Colonel Melchett compare Inspector Slack?

4. Who was Estelle Lestrange's daughter?

5. Who said: "Anyone who murdered Colonel Protheroe would be doing the world at large a service"?

6. Who discovered that Dr. Stone was an impostor?

7. Which character postulated the bizarre theory that people committed crimes because of glandular secretions?

8. Who was in love with Lettice?

9. Which village resident received the obscene phone calls?

10. What problems did the vicar and his wife have with Mary, their housekeeper?

## Clues

1. Why did Miss Marple believe that Anne Protheroe could not have carried a gun with her on the way to the vicarage?

2. What were the three pieces of evidence found in the study?

3. What did Dr. Haydock give as the time of the victim's death?

4. Mrs. Price Ridley's maid, Clara, heard what she thought was a sneeze when she was standing by the front gate at the time of the murder. What was the actual sound she heard?

5. Whose gun was found near the body of the murder victim?

6. How was the vicar lured away from the vicarage prior to the murder?

7. Who was the first suspect to confess to the murder?

8. Who was the second suspect to confess to the murder?

9. What did Miss Marple notice in her garden that put her on the right track?

10. What secret did Griselda wish to keep from her husband?

## Circumstances

1. Why did Colonel Protheroe and Lawrence Redding quarrel?

2. What previous case did Griselda refer to as the one that Miss Marple solved?

3. Why did Griselda sneak off to London on the day of the murder?

4. What did Colonel Protheroe write in his note to the vicar?

5. To what crime did Mr. Hawes want to confess when he tried to telephone the vicarage?

6. How much older was Leonard Clement than his wife, Griselda?

7. Why was the brown suitcase buried in the woods behind the vicarage?

8. Why was the portrait in the attic of the Old Hall slashed?

9. Why did Mrs. Lestrange move to St. Mary Mead?

10. How did Miss Marple know that Mr. Hawes had a medical crisis?

## Quiz 17: *Ordeal by Innocence*

### Characters

1. Of which scientific expedition was Dr. Calgary a member?

2. What type of scientist was Dr. Calgary?

3. Who discovered Rachel Argyle's body?

4. Why was Dr. Calgary not able to testify at Jacko's trial?

5. Who was the first member of the Argyle family to greet Dr. Calgary when he came with his disturbing news?

6. Why was Philip Durrant, Rachel Argyle's son-in-law, confined to a wheelchair?

7. How many children did Rachel and Leo adopt?

8. Who gave an accurate description of the type of murder Jack Argyle was capable of committing?

9. What was Rachel Argyle's main philanthropic interest?

10. Whom did Hester Argyle decide to marry when the mystery was finally solved?

### Clues

1. To which real American murder did Mr. Marshall, the family attorney, refer when conversing with Dr. Calgary about the Argyle case?

2. Who gave Hester the money for gas to attend the play on the night of the murder?

3. Which book of the Bible did Dr. Calgary quote in response to Hester's statement concerning the innocent?

4. Why did the police finally agree to reopen the investigation?

5. Why did Tina, Rachel's adopted daughter, lie about her whereabouts on the night of the murder?

6. How did the position of the magnolia tree on the side of the house incriminate Micky Argyle?

7. Which two clues did Tina utter before she passed out, indicating she knew who the murderer was?

8. Why did Jacko visit his mother on the night of the murder?

9. What was the significance of Jacko's secret wife making her identity known?

10. Why did Micky hate his foster mother, Rachel Argyle?

## Circumstances

1. The Argyle house was renamed when purchased by the Argyle family. What were its original name and new name?

2. Which river isolated the Argyle house from the rest of the town?

3. What were Jack Argyle and Dr. Calgary talking about on the night Jack hitched a ride with the scientist?

4. How did Dr. Calgary learn that Jack had been accused of murder?

5. Why did Leo Argyle and Gwenda postpone their marriage?

6. How did Rachel and Leo come to meet Mary and choose her as their first adopted child?

7. What was the topic of the lecture at Drymouth that Hester and Donald Craig were scheduled to attend on the night Dr. Calgary delivered his shocking news?

8. In what company did Mary and Philip Durrant invest and subsequently lose money?

9. Why did Philip not want to leave the Argyle house even though his wife, Mary, pleaded with him to do so?

10. How did the knife used to stab Tina end up in Micky's pocket?

## Quiz 18: *At Bertram's Hotel*

**Characters**

1. Who owned Bertram's Hotel?

2. For whom was the hotel manager often mistaken?

3. Who was the waiter who served the traditional English tea?

4. What was the name of the Scotland Yard detective who investigated the crimes at the hotel?

5. Who were Elvira Blake's guardians and trustees?

6. What was the name of the forgetful canon who disappeared from Bertram's hotel?

7. What was the name of Elvira's friend who provided her with a smoke screen on several occasions?

8. Why did Bess Sedgwick not want her identity known to her estranged daughter?

9. Whose help did Mrs. McCrae, the canon's housekeeper, solicit when the canon disappeared?

10. What did Ladislaus Malinowski do for a living?

## Clues

1. What did Miss Marple learn when she eavesdropped on Bess Sedgwick and Ladislaus Malinowski's conversation?

2. Why did Elvira visit Mr. Bollard's jewelry store?

3. How many shots were fired when the murder was committed?

4. Whose weapon was found at the murder scene?

5. Which word did Miss Marple use to help the canon remember what happened the night he disappeared?

6. What was the license number of Ladislaus Malinowski's race car?

7. Why did Elvira sneak off to Ireland for a brief visit?

8. Why did Bess Sedgwick threaten to kill Micky Gorman?

9. What crime was committed on the night the canon disappeared?

10. Why was Inspector Davy making inquires at the hotel before the murder was committed?

## Circumstances

1. In what year was Bertram's Hotel remodeled?

2. When did Bertram's Hotel come into existence?

3. For what pastries was Bertram's famous?

4. When did Miss Marple first stay at Bertram's, and with whom?

5. What was the hotel's telephone number?

6. What musical did Colonel Luscombe and Elvira attend?

7. Which modern but unappreciated feature was added to the hotel when it was remodeled?

8. Which movie did the canon see after he realized he would be unable to attend the Congress at Lucerne?

9. Which real London hotel was Bertram's modeled after?

10. Where in London was Bertram's located?

## Quiz 19: *The Body in the Library*

### Characters

1. Who discovered the body in Colonel Bantry's library?

2. Who were the three detectives who investigated the crime?

3. What did Basil Blake do for a living and for what company did he work?

4. What was Ruby Keene's real name?

5. Which character stuttered?

6. Miss Marple severely cross-examined which one of Pamela Reeves's friends during her investigation?

7. What was the name of the hotel where the investigation took place?

8. Why was Conway Jefferson confined to a wheelchair?

9. Who were the two secretly married couples?

10. The vicar's wife, Griselda, announced her pregnancy at the end of *The Murder at the Vicarage*. In *The Body in the Library*, her baby was learning how to crawl. What was the baby's name?

## Clues

1. What interest did Conway Jefferson have in Ruby Keene?

2. Who confessed that she had enough anger to kill Ruby Keene?

3. When Miss Marple examined the body, what did she notice about the victim's fingernails?

4. Who identified Ruby Keene's body?

5. In what was Ruby Keene's dead body wrapped?

6. What did Miss Marple mean when she said that the dress of the victim was all wrong?

7. Whose picture was found in the handbag of Ruby Keene?

8. How did the victim's teeth provide Miss Marple with a clue?

9. Where did Pamela Reeves believe she was going before she was duped and subsequently murdered?

10. How did Miss Marple prove who killed the two victims?

## Circumstances

1. Which model car did George Bartlett drive?

2. What was the name of the quarry where the second body was found?

3. What was the name of the detective story Dolly Bantry was reading on the night of the murder?

4. Whom did Ruby Keene work for before she took the temporary position at the Majestic?

5. For whom did Sir Henry Clithering work before he retired?

6. How did Basil Blake become interested in his profession?

7. How did Josephine break her ankle?

8. Which dance did Josephine and Raymond perform?

9. Which card game were the suspects playing when Ruby failed to keep her appointment?

10. In what time of year was the story set?

## Quiz 20: *Towards Zero*

### Characters

1. Who recited the scenario for a "good detective story"?

2. What were the incidents that led Andrew MacWhirter to attempt suicide?

3. For what sport was Nevile Strange well known?

4. Who believed that taking the law into one's own hands could be justified?

5. How did Audrey, Nevile Strange's first wife, get the scar on her ear?

6. Which one of Superintendent Battle's relatives assisted him with the investigation?

7. From what ailment did Mr. Treves suffer?

8. Who owned the ferry that carted visiters to the Tressilian house?

9. Who was Lady Tressilian's long-time companion?

10. Who prevented Audrey from throwing herself off the cliff?

### Clues

1. How did Don, the dog, give MacWhirter the clue to the killer's identity?

2. Which clue was linked to the dry cleaner in Saltington?

3. Who was the main beneficiary of Lady Tressilian's will?

4. What was the significance of Mr. Treves's story about the two children playing with the bow and arrow?

5. What physical peculiarity did Superintendent Battle notice about Nevile Strange?

6. Why was the "out of order" sign hung on the lift at Balmoral Court?

7. What did MacWhirter see on the night of the murder that caused him to come forward with the information?

8. What was the significance of the long pole on the stairway?

9. What time did the last ferry leave Easterhead?

10. Why did MacWhirter come to Gull's Point looking for a rope, and what was the significance of the rope not having any dust on it?

## Circumstances

1. During which month did the Tressilian family have their family reunion?

2. At what summer resort did the playboy Ted Latimer stay?

3. In which country did Thomas Royde own and operate his plantation?

4. What paralleled the tension at Gull's Point?

5. In which hotel did Mr. Treves stay?

6. What did Superintendent Battle advise Audrey to do after the ordeal was over?

7. To which country was MacWhirter moving to begin his new job?

8. How did Superintendent Battle prove that Ted Latimer could not swim?

9. What did Nevile and his second wife, Kay, fight about on the evening of the murder?

10. Why did Audrey Strange always appear aloof and reserved?

# 3

# The Art of Detection

"His head was exactly the shape of an egg, and he always perched it a little on one side. His mustache was very stiff and military. The neatness of his attire was almost incredible. I believe a speck of dust would have caused him more pain than a bullet wound." Hercule Poirot, the famous Belgian, considered himself "the greatest mind in Europe." His lack of modesty was an integral part of his persona.

"She has remarkable eyesight for her age. She sees everything, and often believes the worst because the worst is often true." A Victorian lady, she indulges in a bit of gossip, but always for a good cause. Most of all, she does not tolerate murder. Miss Jane Marple is Agatha Christie's favorite sleuth.

Her entrance is often preceded by the appearance of one or more apples, either one half eaten perched on a desk or several rolling down the street, having fallen from her car as she opened the door. Mrs. Ariadne Oliver, a mystery writer herself, is believed to be Agatha Christie's alter ego. She appears in seven books, many with Hercule Poirot, and her intuition is invaluable in solving crimes.

Two heads really are better than one. Tommy and Tuppence Beresford, a "typical" English couple living their lives amidst cloak-and-dagger espionage, are partners in crime detection. Their personalities complement one another. Tommy is levelheaded, slow to action, and willing to wait things out. On the other hand, his wife thrives on adventure and does not hesitate to put her plan into motion, often to the surprise of her baffled husband.

Superintendent Battle, Parker Pyne, and Mr. Satterthwaite and Mr. Quin make their appearances in a number of Agatha Christie mysteries and short story collections. Each has his own distinctive flair for detective work and for getting to the "heart" of the matter.

Chapter three contains seven quizzes giving details of the detectives' personality quirks and adorable qualities. How well do you know these master detectives?

## Quiz 21: Too Close for Comfort

In the following twelve hypothetical situations, make the choice that best fits each sleuth's personality.

1. It is a winter's evening and Poirot has invited you to tea. You arrive to find his drawing room
   a. Bright and airy, a window opened to fresh air.
   b. Stifling, a large fire in the grate and the windows closed.
   c. Cold, dark, and damp, a small space heater on low.
   d. Cozy, comfortable, and inviting.

2. You are Miss Marple's doctor and have advised her to give up gardening due to her frail health. How will Miss Marple react to your instructions?
   a. She will ignore your instructions and continue as usual.

b. She will hire an additional man to assist Edwards.

c. She will get a second opinion.

d. She will vicariously enjoy gardening by following Edwards around to see that he prunes properly.

3. You are director of the Paradise Hotel entertainment and have arranged for a walking tour of the island. Hercule Poirot is vacationing and has signed up for the tour. He is the first to arrive and is wearing

a. A black jacket, striped pants, bow tie, and patent leather boots.

b. Safari khakis and expensive hiking boots, latest style.

c. A tux protected by a London Fog trench coat.

d. Bermuda shorts, sports shirt, and sneakers.

4. You are the director of the British Secret Service and send Tommy Beresford on a secret assignment without Tuppence. Tuppence will:

a. Wait patiently for her husband to report back.

b. Don a disguise, invent an assumed name, and devise her own plan.

c. Browbeat Tommy into taking her along in spite of your instructions.

d. Barge into your office and demand that you send both of them or she will not allow her husband to proceed.

5. Hercule Poirot has hired you to decorate his new flat. He has left you with the following decorating suggestions:

a. Museum piece furniture and books arranged alphabetically.

b. The latest style, no matter what it is, and the bookshelves filled with best-sellers.

    c. Square armchairs, rectangular ornaments, horizontal and vertical lines, no curves, and books arranged according to height.

    d. Overstuffed sofa and chairs, leather only, and a collection of historical novels arranged chronologically.

6. You kidnapped Tuppence and sent a ransom note to Tommy demanding 20,000 pounds by midnight or you will dump his wife's lifeless body into the Thames. Tommy's reaction will be to:

    a. Stay calm and develop a plan of action.

    b. Hysterically run to Scotland Yard and demand help.

    c. Leave Tuppence to her own wits. She's gotten out of worse situations.

    d. Pay the ransom and hope for the best.

7. Superintendent Battle easily got you to confess to killing your wife's lover because

    a. Superintendent Battle's interrogations are cruel and abusive and you would confess to anything just to be rid of this man.

    b. He is well trained in modern psychology and he tricked you into a confession by using word associations.

    c. Superintendent Battle never gives up. His fatherly manner and stoic patience caused you to confess. He convinced you that you would feel better if you came clean.

    d. He gathered enough evidence to assure a conviction.

8. The butcher's wife has been murdered and you are assigned to investigate. Failing to turn up suspects,

you visit Miss Marple for advice on how to proceed. Miss Marple suggests that you

a. Look for strangers in the village. They are always up to no good.

b. Listen closely to what the neighbors have to say. They know more than they realize.

c. Study the woman's past and you will surely find enemies.

d. Focus on the husband. So many men have murdered their wives.

9. You are scheduling guest speakers for the upcoming Mystery Writers' Conference and have asked Ariadne Oliver to speak. Her response to your request was:

a. "I will be glad to speak. My lectures are typed and filed. Just give me a topic."

b. "I will speak under one condition—that Hercule Poirot and Jane Marple aren't in attendance."

c. "Get with my secretary and he will arrange everything. I really have no idea what he has planned for me."

D. "I can't give speeches. I get nervous and will probably stammer and look silly. I hate looking silly."

10. Miss Marple is visiting for a fortnight and you offer to cook her favorite breakfast. What would she order?

a. An English muffin, fresh fruit, and black coffee

b. A soft poached egg, fresh rolls, and tea

c. Rye toast, cereal, and a small juice

d. A cheese omelette, crisp bacon, and a tall glass of cold milk

11. You gave a dinner party and invited Mr. Satterthwaite. Upon arrival he scanned the room and took mental note of

    a. Your art collection.

    b. The unaccompanied ladies.

    c. The latest fashions in women's clothing.

    d. The housekeeping abilities of your maid.

12. You answered Mr. Parker Pyne's newspaper ad because you felt that the spark has been extinguished from your marriage. Mr. Parker Pyne agreed to help by

    a. Suggesting you join a ladies' club and volunteer for committee work.

    b. Arranging for you to see a marriage counselor.

    c. Giving your husband lessons on how to be romantic.

    d. Arranging an innocent romance for you to ignite the lost passion.

## Quiz 22: Hercule Poirot, Detective Extraordinaire

Answer fifteen short-answer questions about Hercule Poirot's career, his physical appearance, and his idiosyncrasies.

1. Upon what does M. Poirot rely when solving a mystery?

2. How did Poirot describe his own capabilities as a detective?

3. What feature of his appearance was he most proud of?

4. For whom did he work before he became a private detective?

5. What nationality was Poirot?

6. What religion did Hercule Poirot claim was his?

7. Who was his faithful companion?

8. What was the name of Poirot's man servant?

9. Who was Poirot's secretary?

10. What was Poirot's favorite after-dinner drink?

11. What was his nickname, a name he often used to refer to himself?

12. What color were Poirot's eyes?

13. How tall was Hercule Poirot?

14. What did Poirot use to keep his hair from turning gray?

15. What type of travel did Poirot hate?

## Quiz 23: Miss Jane Marple

The following ten short-answer questions are about Christie's lovable spinster, Miss Marple.

1. To what did Miss Marple attribute her detecting abilities?

2. What analogies does Miss Marple draw to help her solve crimes?

3. Name the village where Miss Marple lived.

4. At what time of the morning did Miss Marple like to start her day?

5. What was Miss Marple's telephone number?

6. What was Miss Marple's mother's name?

7. Who was Miss Marple's cherished nephew?

8. Who was Miss Marple's grandnephew?

9. What color were Miss Marple's eyes?

10. What was the color of her hair?

## Quiz 24: Tommy and Tuppence Beresford

The following quiz consists of ten short-answer questions about this mystery-solving couple. Tommy and Tuppence appeared in five novels, first in 1922 as a young eager duo ready for adventure, and finally in 1974 as a retired but tireless couple, still chasing the bad guys.

1. In what year were Tommy and Tuppence married?

2. How did Tommy and Tuppence make their living?

3. What was the name of the agency Tommy and Tuppence used as a cover?

4. Who were Tommy and Tuppence's sidekick and domestic servant?

5. What was Tuppence's maiden name?

6. What were the names of their twins?

7. What were the names of their grandchildren?

8. Who was Tommy's supervisor?

9. What was the name of the village to which Tommy and Tuppence retired?

10. What was the name and breed of their dog?

## Quiz 25: Mrs. Ariadne Oliver and Mr. Parker Pyne

Mrs. Ariadne Oliver appeared in eight mysteries, usually assisting Poirot in solving a murder. Mr. Parker Pyne was the protagonist in a dozen short stories in which he solved problems of the heart. This quiz contains ten short-answer questions about these two detectives.

1. What types of books did Ariadne Oliver write?

2. What was the name of her protagonist?

3. What was Ariadne Oliver's calling card?

4. What was the color and style of her hair?

5. On what did she rely when solving mysteries?

6. What vices did she claim not to have, but wished she had?

7. What was Mr. Parker Pyne's address?

8. What did Mr. Pyne do before he became a detective?

9. How long did he have his previous position?

10. What was Mr. Parker Pyne's fee for taking a case?

## Quiz 26: Mr. Satterthwaite and Mr. Quin

These two characters appeared in a collection of short stories entitled *The Mysterious Mr. Quin*. The following quiz consists of twelve short answer questions to determine how well you know Mr. Satterthwaite and the enigmatic Mr. Quin.

1. How old was Mr. Satterthwaite in the short story collection *The Mysterious Mr. Quin*?

2. Who was Mr. Satterthwaite's chauffeur?

3. What was Mr. Satterthwaite's favorite vacation spot, and when did he leave for his holiday?

4. What was Mr. Satterthwaite's September and October sporting activity?

5. What was Mr. Satterthwaite's hobby?

6. Why did Mr. Satterthwaite hold fond memories of Kew Gardens?

7. What was Mr. Satterthwaite's main role in life?

8. What was the name of the book Mr. Satterthwaite wrote?

9. Where did Mr. Satterthwaite prefer to spend his time?

10. What was Mr. Quin's first name?

11. Mr. Quin often appeared to be dressed in motley colors, but upon further inspection, such was not the case. What caused this colorful illusion?

12. What was Mr. Quin's profession in "Harlequin's Lane"?

## Quiz 27: Life in the Shadows

This quiz consists of ten short-answer questions to test your knowledge of the secondary characters who lend assistance, support, and flattery to their respective principal counterparts.

1. What was Captain Hastings's first name?

2. What was the name of Captain Hastings's daughter? Hint: She was a murder suspect in Christie's last Poirot mystery.

3. Where did Captain Hastings move when he left England for a brief time?

4. For whom did Hercule Poirot's secretary work before she became employed by Poirot?

5. What did Poirot and his secretary have in common?

6. What did Raymond West do for a living?

7. What did Raymond West's wife do for a living?

8. What was the name of Raymond's wife?

9. What was the name of Superintendent Battle's daughter? Hint: Her odd behavior presented him with a valuable clue in *Towards Zero*.

10. Who was Superintendent Battle's nephew?

# 4

# The Romance Novels of Mary Westmacott

Mary Westmacott, an unknown romance writer, published four books between 1930 and 1947. Her early books portrayed young, naive women struggling for self-identity. As the author matured, so did her heroines. These women, now middle-aged, struggled with midlife crises but learned to accept themselves; they now gave aid and advice to their younger counterparts. Before the publication of Westmacott's fifth novel, the *London Times* spilled the beans and exposed her true identity: Mary Westmacott was the esteemed mystery writer Agatha Christie. After the revelation, she published two more romance novels under her pseudonym.

There has been much speculation about why this successful author chose to publish under an assumed name. A practical reason might be that the romance novel is quite different from the mystery novel. Did she worry whether she would be as successful writing romances as she had been writing mysteries? Would her critics give her new form a fair and unbiased evaluation? This may explain her desire to hide her identity, but once having read these stories, it becomes clear why this shy, private author wrote under a pseudonym. Many struggles portrayed in Christie's romance novels parallel the hardships in her own life. Being an introvert, she may have needed an outlet for expression. Her autobiography is detailed and factual, but lacks emotion. If indeed this theory is true, her romance novels actually provide more details about her childhood and first marriage than her autobiography does.

Chapter four offers nine quizzes that challenge the reader to discover the parallels between fact and fiction.

## Quiz 28: Character Déjà Vu

Interesting characters never die, they just pop up somewhere else. Match these ten Agatha Christie a.k.a. Mary Westmacott romance characters with other fictional characters.

1. Josephine Waite in *Giant's Bread*
2. Joan Scudamore in *Absent in Spring*
3. Nell Vereker in *Giant's Bread*
4. John Gabriel in *The Rose and the Yew Tree*
5. Laura Franklin in *The Burden*
6. Jane Harding in *Giant's Bread*
7. Rupert St. Loo in *The Rose and the Yew Tree*

a. Scarlett O'Hara in *Gone With the Wind*
b. Iago in *Othello*
c. Prince Charming
d. Marquise de Merteuil in *Dangerous Liaisons*
e. Cho-Cho-San in *Madama Butterfly*
f. Violetta in *La Traviata*
g. Anjuli in *The Far Pavilions*
h. Sleeping Beauty
i. Maggie Moran in *Breathing Lessons*

8. Isabella Charteris in
   *The Rose and the Yew
   Tree*
9. Sarah Prentice in *A
   Daughter's a Daughter*
10. Celia in *Unfinished
    Portrait*

j. Daisy Buchanan in
   *The Great Gatsby*

## Quiz 29: Confidants and Accomplices

Many of the characters in Agatha Christie's romance
novels have a special someone with whom they confide or
scheme. This quiz contains ten matching questions from
six Westmacott novels. Match the character with their
confidant.

1. Ann Prentice, *A
   Daughter's a Daughter*
2. Laura Franklin, *The
   Burden*
3. Shirley Franklin, *The
   Burden*
4. Celia, *Unfinished
   Portrait*
5. Vernon Deyre, *Giant's
   Bread*
6. Walter Deyre, *Giant's
   Bread*
7. Myra Deyre, *Giant's
   Bread*
8. Sarah Prentice, *A
   Daughter's a Daughter*
9. Joan Scudamore,
   *Absent in Spring*
10. Isabella Charteris, *The
    Rose and the Yew Tree*

a. Hugh Norreys
b. Nina Anstey
c. "Sasha," Princess
   Hohenbach Salm
d. Sidney Bent
e. Llewellyn Knox
f. J. Larraby
g. Dame Laura
   Whitstable
h. Gerry Lloyd
i. Jane Harding
j. Mr. Baldock

## Quiz 30: Struggle for Survival

Agatha Christie created many of her romance characters to be both vulnerable and strong. In their struggle for happiness and success, they often put up a good fight, but ultimately succumbed to overwhelming negative patterns. Match these ten characters with their emotional burdens.

1. Joan Scudamore, *Absent in Spring*
2. Vernon Deyre, *Giant's Bread*
3. John Gabriel, *The Rose and the Yew Tree*
4. Nell Vereker, *Giant's Bread*
5. Laura Franklin, *The Burden*
6. Ann Prentice, *A Daughter's a Daughter*
7. Jane Harding, *Giant's Bread*
8. Milly Burt, *The Rose and the Yew Tree*
9. Joe Waite, *Giant's Bread*
10. Celia, *Unfinished Portrait*

a. Repetitive pattern of involvement in abusive relationships
b. Blind love for Vernon Deyre
c. Need to protect Milly Burt and destroy Isabella Charteris
d. Need to make lifelong amends to her sister
e. Assumed her life would be like her parents'
f. Need to be safe and financially secure
g. Obsessive love for a woman
h. Need to support the underdog
i. Denial of reality and need to control family
j. Wanting her daughter's happiness over her own

## Quiz 31: *Giant's Bread*

*Giant's Bread* was the first of six romance novels written under Agatha Christie's pseudonym, Mary Westmacott. Longing to write something other than that for which she was known, Christie wrote romances that reflected much of her own life. Quiz four contains ten multiple-choice questions.

1. What was the name of Vernon's family home?
   a. Deyre's Landing
   b. Leeds's Manor
   c. Abbot's Puissant
   d. St. John's Cove

2. What was the "Beast," a frightening symbol from Vernon's childhood?
   a. A wicked tree in the backyard
   b. The neighbor's vicious dog
   c. A grand piano
   d. The dark woods behind the garden

3. What was the main reason that Vernon took a job with his uncle Sidney?
   a. To have enough money to marry
   b. To have enough money to produce his opera
   c. To remain in good standing with his family so that he would not lose his inheritance
   d. To please his possessive mother

4. How did Nell occupy her time while Vernon was in the service?
   a. Nell traveled in America with her family.
   b. Nell did volunteer work at a military hospital.
   c. Nell decorated their new home.
   d. Nell spent most of her time socializing with her old friends in London.

5. Who was the childhood friend who eventually financed Vernon's musical productions?
   a. Sebastian Levine
   b. Joe Waite
   c. Nell Vereker
   d. Uncle Sidney's daughter

6. What was the name of Vernon's first opera?
   a. *Ode to a Woman*
   b. *Eternal Quest*
   c. *The Beast*
   d. *The Prince of the Tower*

7. How did Vernon get amnesia?
   a. Vernon was injured in the war.
   b. Vernon suffered from a severe illness.
   c. Vernon was hit by a car.
   d. Vernon received a head injury in a brawl.

8. Why did Vernon not insist that Nell leave her second husband and return to him?
   a. Vernon assumed she was pregnant.
   b. Vernon realized that he never loved Nell.
   c. Vernon knew he could never provide for her as well as her second husband.
   d. Vernon's music became more important to him.

9. Who did Vernon think he was during the time he had amnesia?
   a. His brother who had died several years earlier
   b. Vernon did not remember anything about his life, so he gave himself a new identity.
   c. His wife's new husband, George Chetwynd
   d. Corporal George Green, a deserter

10. What obstacle did Vernon need to overcome in order
    to be a successful composer?
    a. His fear of failure
    b. His desire for recognition among his peers
    c. Emotional ties with everyone in his life
    d. His desire for a wealthy lifestyle

## Quiz 32: *Unfinished Portrait*

Many of Celia's life trials and tribulations parallel those of
Agatha Christie. This is a story about a young woman's
quest for happiness and self-discovery. If you have read
Agatha Christie's autobiography, you should do well on
this ten-question multiple-choice quiz.

1. How old was Celia when her father died?
   a. Six
   b. Ten
   c. Fourteen
   d. Eighteen

2. How did Celia learn to speak French?
   a. Celia was taught by her lady's maid.
   b. Celia learned French from a neighbor's French
      cousin who visited in the summer.
   c. Celia learned French from her grandmother.
   d. Celia learned French from her governess.

3. In what subject did Celia excel?
   a. Language
   b. Art
   c. Math
   d. Literature

4. Where did Celia go to finish her studies?
   a. France
   b. Germany
   c. Sweden
   d. Italy

5. What character did Celia choose to dress like for the fancy-dress costume ball?
   a. Helen of Troy
   b. Lady Macbeth
   c. Cleopatra
   d. Marguerite from *Faust*

6. What was the name of Celia and Dermont's child?
   a. Rosalind
   b. Jeanne
   c. Judy
   d. Miriam

7. What was the name of Celia's first book?
   a. *The Gun Man*
   b. *Open Enemy*
   c. *The Obstacle*
   d. *Lonely Harbour*

8. What other tragedy occurred at the time Celia's marriage failed?
   a. Celia's mother died.
   b. Celia's child became very ill.
   c. Celia's family home burned.
   d. Bad investments caused Celia to lose trust in everyone.

9. Why did Dermont want a divorce?
   a. Dermont could not deal with Celia's depression.
   b. Dermont felt that married life was too confining.

c. Dermont fell in love with another woman.

d. Dermont never really loved Celia.

10. What did Celia's publisher believe was the strongest feature of her writing?

a. Clear characterizations

b. Good storytelling

c. Superb detailing

d. Compelling plots

## Quiz 33: *Absent in Spring*

Agatha Christie/Mary Westmacott wrote *Absent in Spring* in 1944. The protagonist, Joan Scudamore, was stranded at a traveler's rest house in Mesopotamia. Isolated, she began reflecting on her life and her relationships. Quiz six contains ten multiple-choice questions.

1. What was the purpose of Joan's trip to this desolate part of the world?

a. Joan needed time away from her home and family to reflect on her life.

b. Joan was going to visit her ill daughter, who was living in the Middle East.

c. Joan was to join an old friend for a reunion and holiday.

d. Joan was trying to locate her estranged sister.

2. What was the significance of Joan's running into an old school friend while waiting at the first rest house?

a. Their meeting was the catalyst that caused Joan to reflect on her life.

b. The meeting made Joan realize how alone she really was.

c. The meeting caused Joan to change her travel plans, which started a chain of unforeseen events.

    d. Joan's friend hinted that Joan's husband was having an affair.

3. What was Joan's analogy for the truth as it crept to the surface?
    a. A monster raising its ugly head
    b. A light at the end of the tunnel
    c. A white flag of freedom
    d. Lizards popping out from everywhere

4. What was the headmistress's advice to Joan when she graduated?
    a. Learn to recognize the truth among all misconceptions.
    b. Do not accept things at face value just because it is the easiest way to live life.
    c. Do not judge others by your own standards.
    d. There is more than one truth; look for the truth in everyone.

5. In the beginning of her isolation, what did Joan do to handle her idle time?
    a. Joan stayed in bed and slept.
    b. Joan cleaned her dusty hotel room.
    c. Joan visited with the cook and helped out in the kitchen.
    d. Joan recited poetry to herself.

6. How did Joan's family view her as a wife and mother?
    a. Joan was very controlling and in denial of her family's problems.
    b. Joan would always be there to solve all their problems.
    c. Joan suspected ulterior motives and often misunderstood her family.

    d. Joan was too busy with her own life to recognize the needs of her family.

7. What nickname did Joan's husband, Rodney Scudamore, have for his wife?
    a. Little Mother
    b. Angel
    c. Little jumping Joan
    d. Kitten

8. How did Joan's oldest daughter, Averil, react to Joan's invitation to dinner?
    a. Averil refused to see her mother.
    b. Averil was anxious to see her mother, because she noticed a change in Joan.
    c. Averil insisted that she bring along her husband for moral support.
    d. Averil hoped for a reconciliation.

9. What was the result of Joan's transformation?
    a. When Joan returned home, she made amends to her family.
    b. Joan immediately confronted Rodney about the alleged affair.
    c. Joan's good intentions faded as soon as she arrived home.
    d. Joan and Rodney had their first heart-to-heart talk.

10. From where did Christie take the title, *Absent in Spring*?
    a. A poem by Shelley
    b. A poem by Elizabeth Barrett Browning
    c. A Shakespearean sonnet
    d. A sonnet by Tennyson

## Quiz 34: *The Rose and the Yew Tree*

Agatha Christie finally wrote *The Rose and the Yew Tree* in 1947 after nurturing the story for over twenty years. The following quiz consists of ten multiple-choice questions.

1. What was the name of the village in which the story took place?
   a. St. Cloud
   b. St. Johns
   c. St. Mary
   d. St. Loo

2. How did Hugh Norreys become a cripple?
   a. Hugh was wounded in World War II.
   b. Hugh was a victim of polio.
   c. Hugh was hit by a drunk driver.
   d. Hugh was shot in a hunting accident.

3. What was Hugh's profession before his accident?
   a. Hugh was a minister.
   b. Hugh was a naval commander.
   c. Hugh was a gamekeeper.
   d. Hugh was a schoolmaster.

4. With whom did Hugh live and who was his caretaker?
   a. His cousin
   b. His sister
   c. His nurse
   d. His housekeeper

5. Of which political party was John Gabriel a member?
   a. The Liberal party
   b. The Conservative Party
   c. The Socialist party
   d. The Communist party

6. What heroic deed did John Gabriel perform to further his political career?
   a. John rescued several children from a concentration camp during the war.
   b. John aided the police in capturing an escaped criminal who was holding several people hostage.
   c. John jumped into the harbor to save a drowning child even though he could not swim.
   d. John fought for the rights of a poor, elderly woman who was being evicted from her residence because she could not pay her rent.

7. What was John Gabriel's ulterior motive in running for office?
   a. He was power hungry.
   b. He wanted a cushy job.
   c. He was dedicated to serving the public.
   d. He wanted to raise his status in the community.

8. Why did John Gabriel befriend Milly Burt?
   a. Milly lost her position and was destitute.
   b. John took pity on her because of her abusive husband.
   c. Milly had an illegitimate chi'ld and was chastised by the community.
   d. Milly was accused of committing a crime that she did not commit.

9. Who rescued Milly Burt and saved John Gabriel's campaign?
   a. Hugh Norreys
   b. Mrs. Carslake
   c. Mrs. Bigham Charteris
   d. Lady Tressilian

10. What turned John Gabriel around and caused him to dedicate his life to the unfortunate?
    a. A near-death experience
    b. Losing his political career
    c. Isabella's unselfish love
    d. Losing his wealth

## Quiz 35: *A Daughter's a Daughter*

Written in 1952, *A Daughter's a Daughter* describes the love/hate relationship between a mother and her daughter; and their ultimate liberation from one another. This quiz contains ten multiple-choice questions.

1. Where was Sarah vacationing when Ann fell in love and became engaged?
    a. America
    b. India
    c. France
    d. Switzerland

2. How did Dame Laura Whitstable think people should become acquainted with themselves?
    a. By keeping a journal and reviewing it on the last day of the year
    b. By spending a month alone in the middle of the desert
    c. By paying attention to young children's actions
    d. By meditating every morning before starting the day

3. What was the name of the radio show Laura hosted?
    a. "How to Be Alive Today"
    b. "Women in the New Generation"

   c. "Girl Talk"

   d. "Liberations of the Modern Woman"

4. Where did Gerry go when he struck out on his own?
   a. To India to run a tea plantation
   b. To Australia to start a shipping business
   c. To South Africa to grow oranges
   d. To America to farm cotton

5. What was Richard's solution to the problems between him and Sarah?
   a. To postpone his and Ann's wedding until Sarah married
   b. To insist that Sarah move out and find a place of her own
   c. To send Sarah on an adventure around the world
   d. To send Sarah to live with relatives in France during the first six months of his marriage to Ann

6. How many times had Sarah's husband been married before?
   a. Four
   b. Two
   c. Three
   d. Five

7. Other than missing the life of luxury, why was Sarah afraid to leave her husband?
   a. Sarah was afraid that she could not live on her own.
   b. Sarah knew her mother would not let her come back home to live.
   c. Sarah was too proud to admit that the marriage was a mistake.
   d. Sarah was addicted to cocaine, and her husband provided the finances for her habit.

8. Who convinced Sarah to leave her husband?
   a. Gerry Lloyd, an old boyfriend
   b. Dame Whitstable
   c. Edith, the doting housekeeper
   d. Sarah's grandmother

9. How did Ann deal with her loss of Richard?
   a. Ann isolated herself and refused to socialize with anyone.
   b. Ann refused to see her daughter, Sarah.
   c. Ann traded her quiet life for the party life.
   d. Ann married the man she had dated before she met Richard.

10. Why did Ann not object to Sarah's marriage?
    a. Ann felt that if Sarah left home, Richard would come back.
    b. She knew Sarah would be unhappy and wanted revenge because Sarah had ruined Ann's life with Richard.
    c. She didn't think Sarah would really go through with the marriage.
    d. She knew that once Sarah made up her mind, it could not be changed.

## Quiz 36: *The Burden*

*The Burden* was the last of the Christie/Westmacott romance novels. As in many of her romance stories, the theme is love and sacrifice. This ten-question multiple-choice quiz details the relationship between two sisters and their intertwined lives.

1. How did Laura and Mr. Baldock become friends?
   a. Mr. Baldock took pity on Laura and invited her for tea.
   b. Mr. Baldock agreed to look in on Laura from time to time while her parents were away.
   c. Laura began visiting Mr. Baldock when he was ill.
   d. Laura kept Mr. Baldock company while he puttered in his garden.

2. What was Mr. Baldock's profession?
   a. Mr. Baldock was a writer.
   b. Mr. Baldock was a retired general.
   c. Mr. Baldock was a history professor.
   d. Mr. Baldock was the town magistrate.

3. What incident transformed Laura into a loving, protective sister?
   a. Laura saved Shirley's life when the house caught on fire.
   b. Shirley caught pneumonia and almost died.
   c. Shirley was lost in the woods behind their house for two days.
   d. Laura had a dream that Shirley died.

4. What was Shirley's dream?
   a. To live in a castle by the sea
   b. To marry and have many children
   c. To live in a small country village and dedicate her life to her husband's career
   d. To live on an island in a white house with green shutters and do nothing all day

5. What career did Llewellyn give up when he received his calling to become an evangelist?
   a. Finance
   b. Medicine
   c. Architecture
   d. Geology

6. What were Llewellyn's three visions?
   a. His wedding date, the birth of his first child, and the day of his death
   b. A sinking ship, a foggy morning on the moors, and a burning house
   c. An owlish-looking man sitting at a gigantic desk, a sanitarium surrounded by pine trees, and the face of a suffering woman
   d. A veiled lady in white, a preacher, and a funeral

7. Where was Llewellyn when he received his calling?
   a. Caught in an avalanche while skiing
   b. At his mother's funeral
   c. In a hospital recovering from a riding accident
   d. Camping alone in the desert

8. Why was Shirley unhappily married to her second husband even though he fulfilled her dream?
   a. Laura had given up her own happiness for Shirley's sake.
   b. Shirley realized she loved her first husband.
   c. Shirley's second husband turned out to be an alcoholic.
   d. Life was no longer a challenge.

9. What shade of lipstick did Laura choose for her dinner date with Llewellyn?
   a. Fatal Apple
   b. Pale Pink
   c. Bold Red
   d. Innocent Blush

10. What did Shirley's death personally mean to Laura?
    a. That Laura was now free to marry
    b. That Shirley took Laura's secret to the grave
    c. That Shirley paid for Laura's sin and canceled the debt between them
    d. That Laura could be her own person rather than Shirley's caretaker

# 5

# Short, Sweet, and Deadly

Agatha Christie wrote fifteen short story collections. Many of these collections featured her most popular detective, Hercule Poirot, showing his lack of humility by accepting only the most challenging cases. Miss Marple also performed some delightful sleuthing in the collection *Tuesday Club Murders* (1932), and Tommy and Tuppence Beresford appeared in a collection entitled *Partners in Crime* (1929). In the personal ads of the daily paper, Mr. Parker Pyne asked: "Are you happy? If not, consult Mr. Parker Pyne, 17 Richmond Street." This simple ad landed the detective a dozen bizarre cases involving some rather humorous clients, in the collection *Mr. Parker Pyne, Detective*. With *The Hound of Death* (1933), Christie created a collection of macabre ghost stories featuring protagonists gifted with second sight and other ghostly talents. Even though these stories are indeed short, they are nevertheless as tricky as her full-length novels.

Chapter five contains thirteen quizzes examining these short mysteries. Several short stories appear in more than one collection. There is at least one trivia question for each short story. Set your timer and begin.

## Quiz 37: *The Adventure of Christmas Pudding and a Selection of Entrees* and *Double Sin and Other Stories*

Quiz thirty-seven contains twelve multiple-choice questions on the short stories appearing in two collections, *The Adventure of Christmas Pudding and a Selection of Entrees,* and *Double Sin and Other Stories.* The original stories were published in magazines as early as 1920. The collections were published in 1960 and 1961.

1. What was the cryptic message Poirot found in his room in the short story "The Adventure of Christmas Pudding"?
   a. "GO AWAY, YOU ARE NOT WANTED HERE."
   b. "BEWARE, DESMOND LEE-WORTLEY IS AN IMPOSTOR."
   c. "DON'T EAT NONE OF THE PLUM PUDDING. ONE AS WISHES YOU WELL."
   d. "SHE AIN'T REALLY HIS SISTER."

2. What was hidden in the chest in "The Mystery of the Spanish Chest"?
   a. The silver candlestick used as the murder weapon
   b. The missing eighteenth-century Spanish paintings
   c. A bloodstained rug used to transport the murder victim
   d. The body of Mr. Clayton

3. Who asked Poirot for help in solving the murder in "The Under Dog"?
   a. Lady Astwell, the victim's wife
   b. Lily Margrave, Lady Astwell's paid companion
   c. Charles Leverson, the victim's nephew
   d. Captain Humphrey Naylor

4. What was Poirot asked to return to the butler in the short story "The Dream"?
   a. The suicide note
   b. The original will leaving everything to the butler
   c. The letter from Mr. Farley requesting his advice
   d. The message warning him to leave Northway House

5. What remark did Miss Greenshaw make before she was murdered that led Miss Marple to suspect the truth in "Greenshaw's Folly"?
   a. "If I died without a will, I suppose that son of a horse coper would get it."
   b. "Beneficiary to a will mustn't witness it. That's right, isn't it?"
   c. "Now that I think of it, a couple of strange visitors are just what we need, aren't they, Miss Cresswell?"
   d. "If you want to know the time, ask a policeman.

**From *Double Sin and Other Stories:***

6. Why did Mary Durrant seek Poirot and Hastings's help in the short story "Double Sin"?
   a. To find out who was following her
   b. Her luggage containing expensive miniatures was taken.
   c. To find out if her fiancé was an impostor
   d. To locate her missing twin sister

7. Why did Hercule Poirot pay a surprise visit to the home of John Harrison in "Wasps' Nest"?
   a. To prevent a murder
   b. To deliver the ransom for his kidnapped niece
   c. To find out who was trying to poison him
   d. To prevent a potential suicide

8. "The Theft of the Royal Ruby" was published under a different title in a collection of the same name. What was that title?
   a. "The Adventure of Christmas Pudding"
   b. "The Incredible Theft"
   c. "The Red Signal"
   d. "The Four Suspects"

9. What was the secret of Alicia Coombe's doll in "The Dressmaker's Doll"?
   a. The doll wanted to be loved.
   b. The doll belonged to Alicia's mother.
   c. The doll possessed strange powers.
   d. The doll resembled Alicia's deceased daughter.

10. Why did Marcus Hardman call upon Hercule Poirot in the short story "The Double Clue"?
    a. To find a hidden map that led to his uncle's will
    b. To find his estranged wife
    c. To be a pawn in a murder plot
    d. To recover his stolen jewelry collection

11. Why did Madame Simone Daubreuil wish to give up her contact with the spirit world?
    a. Madame Simone's husband, Raoul Daubreuil, did not approve.
    b. The ordeal was becoming physically draining.
    c. She feared she would not return from the spirit world.
    d. She was beginning to loose touch with reality.

12. What did the vicar's wife, Bunch Harman, find in church one morning that led her to Miss Marple for help in the story "Sanctuary"?
    a. A ransom note
    b. A suitcase containing love letters

c. A dying man

d. An abandoned infant

## Quiz 38: *Dead Man's Mirror* or *Murder in the Mews*

*Dead Man's Mirror*, the American title, or *Murder in the Mews*, its British counterpart, is a collection of four novellas: "Dead Man's Mirror," "Murder in the Mews," "The Incredible Theft," and "Triangle at Rhodes." The following ten questions ask you to name the novella.

1. Which novella was not published in the American collection?

2. "The Second Gong" was expanded to become which novella?

3. Which novella was very similar in setting and situation to *Evil Under the Sun*?

4. In which novella was a murder made to look like a suicide?

5. In which novella was a suicide made to look like a murder?

6. Christie quoted a Tennyson poem, "The Lady of Shalott," in which novella?

7. Lady Cheveniz-Gore believed she was the reincarnation of Hatshepsut in which novella?

8. In which novella did the murder take place on Guy Fawkes Day?

9. In which novella did Hercule Poirot refer to stereotypes and trace a warning in the sand?

10. Which story featured a crime other than a murder?

## Quiz 39: *The Golden Ball and Other Stories* and *The Listerdale Mystery*

This quiz consists of fifteen multiple choice questions. The first nine questions are from stories in *The Golden Ball and Other Stories*. The last six are from *The Listerdale Mystery*.

From *The Golden Ball and Other Stories:*

1. Who was the mysterious girl George Rowland encountered on the train in the short story "The Girl on the Train"?
   a. A Baltic spy smuggling war secrets
   b. A grand duchess trying to escape a forced marriage
   c. A bored country lady seeking adventure
   d. A schoolgirl running away from an overbearing guardian

2. What new purchase gave Edward Robinson a sense of freedom and adventure in "The Manhood of Edward Robinson"?
   a. Shares in a race horse
   b. A house in the country
   c. A small two-seater sports car
   d. A ticket on the Orient Express

3. For what job did Count Streptitch hire Jane Cleveland in "Jane in Search of a Job"?
   a. An undercover detective to find the stolen jewels of a royal family
   b. A governess for a spoiled princess
   c. A secretary to accompany him on his travels to India
   d. An impersonator of a grand duchess who was fearful of being kidnapped

4. What did Dorothy and Ted discover in their basket of cherries in "A Fruitful Sunday"?
   a. A stolen ruby necklace worth 50,000 pounds
   b. A single ruby
   c. An imitation stone necklace
   d. A diamond ring

5. What test did any potential husband of Mary Montresor's have to pass before she would consider accepting his marriage proposal in "The Golden Ball"?
   a. That he was not the jealous type
   b. That he could be responsible with money
   c. That he could stand up to her tyrannical father
   d. That he could behave courageously in an emergency

6. How did the emerald get into the pocket of James's trousers in "The Rajah's Emerald"?
   a. A thief slipped it into the pocket while James was bathing.
   b. The trousers James wore were not his.
   c. The emerald was placed there when the trousers were sent out for cleaning.
   d. A beautiful stranger slipped it into his pocket while they were dancing.

7. In what opera did Paula Nazorkoff revenge her lover's death and sing her own farewell in "Swan Song"?
   a. *Madama Butterfly*
   b. *Tosca*
   c. *Rigoletto*
   d. *La Traviata*

8. Why did Theo Darrell leave her lover and return to her husband in "Magnolia Blossom"?
   a. Her husband's company was headed for financial ruin and she could not abandon him during this ordeal.
   b. The guilt was too overwhelming.
   c. Her husband discovered he had a fatal illness.
   d. Her husband threatened to ruIn her lover.

9. How did Joyce Lambert get her dog, Terry, in "Next to a Dog"?
   a. Terry was a stray she found on the street.
   b. A neighbor had to give him up because the neighbor was leaving the country.
   c. Terry was a Christmas present from an old lover.
   d. Terry was a gift from her brother.

From *The Listerdale Mystery:*

10. How was the destitute widow Mrs. St. Vincent able to afford an expensive, completely staffed cottage in "The Listerdale Mystery"?
    a. An unknown benefactor paid the rent and upkeep.
    b. The owner was more interested in having a good tenant than in making money.
    c. The rent was very low because the house was haunted.
    d. The rent was very low because a murder was committed there and the body was hidden somewhere within.

11. Why did Alix Martin become suspicious of her new husband in "Philomel Cottage"?
    a. Alix found a letter from her husband's ex-lover.
    b. Alix suspected her husband of being an escaped wife-killer.
    c. Alix found poison in her husband's drawer.
    d. Alix caught her husband hiding a gun under the mattress.

12. Why did Magdalen Vaughan appeal to Sir Edward Palliser to help her find her aunt's murderer in "Sing a Song of Sixpence"?
    a. Sir Edward was the family solicitor and the only person Magdalen trusted.
    b. Magdalen found Sir Edward's name among her aunt's personal papers.
    c. Magdalen and Sir Edward had a romantic interlude ten years before and, upon separation, he pledged his eternal service.
    d. Sir Edward was the only person who believed that Magdalen was innocent of her aunt's murder.

13. In the short story "Accident," why was Inspector Evans suspicious of Mrs. Merrowdene?
    a. He suspected her of killing her previous husband.
    b. He suspected her of being an escapee from a nearby prison.
    c. He caught Mrs. Merrowdene in one too many lies.
    d. He spied her in a clandestine meeting with a convicted murderer.

14. In the short story "Mr. Eastwood's Adventure," Mr. Eastwood mentions the name of one of Agatha Christie's plays. What was the name of this play adapted from her book *Mrs. McGinty's Dead*?
    a. *Murder Ahoy!*

   b. *Alibi*
   c. *Murder Most Foul*
   d. *Black Coffee*

15. What real event in Christie's life inspired one of the stories in this collection?
   a. Desperately looking for employment inspired "Jane in Search of a Job"
   b. Buying a sports car inspired "The Manhood of Edward Robinson"
   c. Buying a cottage two miles away from the nearest village inspired "Philomel Cottage"
   d. Leaving a country dance with a total stranger inspired "The Golden Ball"

## Quiz 40: *The Hound of Death and Other Stories*

This collection of short stories deals with supernatural forces and twists of fate. Match the story with the description.

   1. "The Hound of Death"

   a. Distress calls from the golf course led Jack to believe that his mind was playing tricks on him. He was tricked, but not by his mind.

   2. "The Red Signal"

   b. Mrs. Lancaster was not afraid to move into a haunted house. This made the lonely ghost very happy.

   3. "The Fourth Man"

   c. Did a Belgian nun have supernatural powers, or was it just spontaneous human combustion?

4. "The Gipsy"

d. The law said that a woman cannot testify against her husband, but what if she wanted to?

5. "The Lamp"

e. Motherly love was too great a power for the medium, Simone. Her contact with the other world became her last.

6. "Wireless"

f. A young heir came into his title and estate, but a greedy stepmother's supernatural powers left him behaving like a feline.

7. "Witness for the Prosecution"

g. Was this a case of multiple personalities or a masterful plan of revenge?

8. "The Mystery of the Blue Jar"

h. A motorist, stranded on the Wiltshire Downs, took refuge in a nice family's cozy home. Once inside, he began receiving distress signals; the skeletons would not stay in the closet.

9. "The Strange Case of Sir Arthur Carmichael"

i. Was Mrs. Harter receiving messages from her dead husband telling her to be ready for his arrival to take her to the other side, or was she being rushed to the grave by an earthly power?

10. "The Call of the Wings"

j. Dickie Lawes's childhood nightmares became reality and were occurring in his adult life.

11. "The Last Séance"

k. Silas Hamer was willing to pay any price for peace of mind.

12. "SOS"

l. Strong signals warned the protagonist of imminent danger.

## Quiz 41: *The Labors of Hercules*

This Hercule Poirot short story collection by Christie was patterned after the twelve exploits of Hercules, the strong man, in the Greek myths. Match the plots with their stories named after these mythical labors.

1. "Nemean Lion"

a. Poirot was assigned to find and return a stolen painting depicting characters of "rich, voluptuous flesh."

2. "The Lernean Hydra"

b. Poirot was trying to locate a graceful, doelike dancer who had "hair like wings of gold."

3. "The Arcadian Deer"

C. Poirot was tracing a Renaissance goblet

that had been stolen. His intention was not to return it to the owner, but to the nuns to whom it had been entrusted.

4. "The Erymanthian Boar"

d. Poirot was hired to find the source of a multiheaded monster of gossip and rumor.

5. "The Augean Stables"

e. Poirot was in charge of cleaning up a political scandal about to be revealed by a seedy tabloid.

6. "The Stymphalean Birds"

f. Poirot busted a cocaine ring that was exploiting young girls.

7. "The Cretan Bull"

g. Poirot was assigned to locate a kidnapped Pekingese.

8. "The Horses of Diomedes"

h. Poirot captured two raptorlike women who preyed upon innocent victims by blackmail.

9. "The Girdle of Hyppolita"

i. Poirot lured a vicious guard dog out of a cellar nightclub named Hell.

10. "The Flock of Geryon"

j. Poirot captured an unsavory, vicious gambling lord.

11. "The Apples of the Hesperides"

k. Poirot saved a muscular, godlike young man from destruction.

12. "The Capture of Cer-
    berus"

    l. Poirot freed a group of
    wealthy widows under
    the influence of a
    greedy evangelist.

## Quiz 42: *The Mysterious Mr. Quin*

Mr. Quin and Mr. Satterthwaite makes their appearance
in this Hitchcock-type collection of short stories. Select
the correct choices in this quiz.

1. How did Mr. Quin come to attend the fireside gathering at Royston Hall on New Year's Eve in "The
   Coming of Mr. Quin"?
   a. Lady Laura invited him.
   b. Mr. Quin's car broke down near the estate.
   c. Mr. Quin came at Mr. Satterthwaite's request.
   d. Eleanor Portal requested his assistance.

2. In "The Shadow on the Glass," Mr. Quin asked Mr.
   Satterthwaite to give his strongest impression of the
   double murder. What was Mr. Satterthwaite's reply?
   a. "The time the shots were fired"
   b. "The sight of the dead bodies"
   c. "The blood spot on Mrs. Scott's ear"
   d. "The pistol in Mrs. Staverton's hand"

3. In "At the Bells and Motley," Mr. Satterthwaite, in
   solving the murder, referred to Mr. Quin as
   a. A man of magic
   b. The invisible one
   c. A thin, dark man
   d. A matchmaker

4. What was the name of the restaurant/hotel that Mr. Quin and Mr. Satterthwaite often visited, which was first mentioned in "The Sign in the Sky"?
   a. Pagliacci's
   b. The Harlequin
   c. Abbot's Mede
   d. Arlecchino

5. How did Mr. Quin gather the necessary people at the Bohemian cage, Le Caveau, in "The Soul of the Croupier"?
   a. Mr. Quin sent everyone pieces of a riddle.
   b. Mr. Quin suggested a "Hedges and Highways" party.
   c. Mr. Quin had Mr. Satterthwaite hand-deliver the invitations.
   d. Mr. Quin sent his chauffeur to collect everyone.

6. What was Mr. Cosden's unachieved desire in "The Man from the Sea"?
   a. To make his fortune by the age of forty or give up
   b. To marry the first woman he fell in love with
   c. To trust no one, especially when it came to love and money
   d. To build a house, plant a tree, and have a son

7. In "The Voice in the Dark," what was the ghostly warning of Abbot's Mede Hall?
   a. "Give back what is not yours. Give back what you have stolen."
   b. "I know who you are. Your secret will be revealed."
   c. "It is your turn to die. You must pay for your sin."
   d. "The blood on your hands will haunt you forever."

8. In "The Faces of Helen," what physical effect was the prelude to an attempted murder?
   a. Centripetal motion, which keeps objects from flying into space
   b. Gravity, a force that pulls an object to earth
   c. Resonance, a high-pitched note that can shatter glass
   d. Magnetism, a force that attracts iron or steel to a body

9. In "The Dead Harlequin," whom did the harlequin in Frank Bristow's painting resemble?
   a. The murder victim, Lord Charnley
   b. Mr. Quin
   c. The murderer
   d. Mr. Satterthwaite

10. In "The Bird with the Broken Wing," Christie surreptitiously mentioned the title of one of her mysteries. What was the name of this novel?
    a. *Towards Zero*
    b. *Crooked House*
    c. *Death Comes as the End*
    d. *N or M?*

11. In "The World's End," Mr. Satterthwaite gave up the comforts of the Riviera to accompany a friend to Corsica. Who was this friend?
    a. The Duchess of Leith
    b. Mr. Quin
    c. A princess from his past
    d. Lady Cynthia Drage

12. What was at the end of Mr. Quin's lane in "Harlequin's Lane"?
    a. A folly
    b. A rubbish heap
    c. A cliff where lovers leap
    d. A grassy meadow

## Quiz 43: *Mr. Parker Pyne, Detective*

In this collection of twelve short stories, Mr. Parker Pyne claimed he was a doctor of the heart rather than a detective. In the first six stories, Mr. Pyne solved the personal problems of six unhappy clients who answered his newspaper ad. The next six stories took place around Middle Eastern and North African historical sites while Mr. Pyne was on holiday. The problems in these last six stories are more sinister in nature and the characters were not always grateful for Mr. Pyne's assistance. Match each summary to its story title.

### Part One

1. "The Case of the Middle-Aged Wife"

2. "The Case of the Discontented Soldier"

a. Mr. Wade had six months to win back his wife. Was Mr. Pyne successful, or did he have another problem to solve?

b. Mrs. Packington could not sit by and watch her husband waltz out of her life. At Mr. Pyne's advice, she changed her focus and filled up her own dance card.

**Part Two**

Petra. This historic setting lent itself to thievery once again.

2. "The Gate of Baghdad"

b. Blackmail led a husband to steal. Mr. Parker Pyne convinced the young man to go straight to his wife and confess the truth, but not the whole truth. After all, wouldn't a wife prefer a Don Juan for a husband over a fool?

3. "The House of Shiraz"

c. He wanted the money *and* the girl. Murder was not too high a price to pay. This story took place on the *S.S. Fayoum* as it floated past the temples of Karnak.

4. "The Pearl of Price"

d. Mr. Parker Pyne was visiting the site near Damascus where St. Paul was lowered out of a window. The site was now a setting for masterful deception, but Mr. Parker Pyne was too smart for the criminal.

5. "Death on the Nile"

e. A long way from home, Mr. Parker Pyne visited the rock of Behistun. But even on this sojourn he brought along a clipping from the newspaper that included his famous ad. This was his ticket to righting a wrong and freeing an innocent actress.

6. "The Oracle of Delphi"

f. Mr. Parker Pyne was determined to continue on his Greek holiday unrecognized. His plan was more than successful when the villain donned an all-too-familiar disguise.

## Quiz 44: *Partners in Crime*

This collection of episodes features Tommy and Tuppence Beresford solving a variety of cases. In each situation they pretended to be fictional sleuths of other detective-story writers. In this ten-question quiz, match the sleuth with the short story from the *Partners in Crime* series.

1. "The Adventure of the Sinister Stranger"
2. "Finessing the King"
3. "The Case of the Missing Lady"
4. "Blindman's Buff"
5. "The Crackler"

a. Hanaud
b. Thornley Colton, the blind detective
c. Inspector French
d. McCarty and Riordan
e. Francis and Desmond Okewood

6. "The Sunningdale Mystery"
7. "The House of Lurking Death"
8. "The Clergyman's Daughter"
9. "The Ambassador's Boots"
10. "The Unbreakable Alibi"

f. Miss Polly Burton
g. Sherlock Holmes
h. Edgar Wallace
i. Dr. Fortune and Superintendent Bell
j. Roger Sheringham

## Quiz 45: *Poirot Investigates*

This quiz contains fourteen clues written in verse. Match the correct short story title to each clue.

### Clues

1. To New York the bonds sailed, there to be sold,
   But the package had vanished, or so we were told.
   Two boats crossed the Atlantic on that fateful day,
   One carrying bonds, the other dismay.

2. Twenty-four and a quarter hours was all Poirot had
   To discover Mr. MacAdam, alive or dead.
   Daniels or Murphy? Who had the traitor's notion?
   The answer—mal de mer—lay across the ocean.

3. A murder avenged, years after the fact.
   When opportunity knocked, the avenger did act.
   The lesson here: beware those you hurt,
   For you may receive your own just "dessert."

4. Three men for dinner; is that really true?
   One man is dead. Where's the other two?
   The clue's in the food uneaten that night.
   The rice souffle, untouched; for he could not eat one
   more bite.

5. One diamond or two
   Will give you the clue
   To solve the case
   Of Yardly Chase.

6. Excavations in Egypt uncovered a king's tomb.
   The result: superstition, murder, and doom.
   Poirot across the sea, Hastings did coax
   To visit the desert and uncover the hoax.

7. A romantic letter, a lady in distress—
   Poirot snooped all night without any rest.
   This lady was a fraud, but the game Poirot played,
   For it was the shoes that gave her away.

8. Word association reveals the plot.
   Suicide or accident, it surely is not.
   A greedy young wife, a dastardly deed,
   She murdered for money, but didn't succeed.

9. Japp bet Poirot a fiver to solve the case
   From his own comfy chair in his own tidy place.
   The facts were presented and were all he did need
   To find the missing man and the doer of the deed.

10. A bearded stranger arrived
    And a rich uncle died.
    Poirot unraveled the tale
    Using clues sent by mail.

11. Wit versus brains, a search for what's mine.
    Will Poirot find the proof? It's a race against time.
    My uncle was smart and set in his ways,
    But educating a woman sometimes pay.

12. The weekend at Brighton at Hastings's expense
    Was all but relaxing. It grew a bit tense.
    Mrs. Opalsen's pearls were out on the lam,
    But Poirot's to the rescue at the Metropolitan.

13. Four hundred forty-four pounds, four and fourpence
    Gave ol' Poirot a tidy little balance.
    But watch for sure things and always know their yields,
    And never, never invest in Porcupine oilfields.

14. A Montagu flat, sublet for eighty pounds,
    Was far below price for the high part of town.
    The landlords were spies, and their trail was hot.
    They must lease their place to avoid being caught.

## Titles

a. "The Adventure of 'The Western Star'"

b. "The Tragedy at Marsdon Manor"

c. "The Adventure of the Cheap Flat"

d. "The Mystery of Hunter's Lodge"

e. "The Million-Dollar Bond Robbery"

f. "The Adventure of the Egyptian Tomb"

g. "The Jewel Robbery at the Grand Metropolitan"

h. "The Kidnapped Prime Minister"

i. "The Disappearance of Mr. Davenheim"

j. "The Adventure of the Italian Nobleman"

k. "The Case of the Missing Will"

l. "The Veiled Lady"

m. "The Lost Mine"

n. "The Chocolate Box"

## Quiz 46: *The Regatta Mystery and Other Stories*

*The Regatta Mystery and Other Stories* is a collection of short stories featuring M. Hercule Poirot, Miss Jane Marple, and Mr. Parker Pyne. Quiz forty-six contains ten short-answer questions.

1. What was the name of Isaac Pointz's stolen diamond in "The Regatta Mystery"?

2. Who investigated the missing diamond in "The Regatta Mystery"?

3. According to Hercule Poirot in "The Mystery of the Baghdad Chest," to which three people should women always tell the truth?

4. What asymmetrical design clued Hercule Poirot to the solution of the crime in "How Does Your Garden Grow?"

5. In "Problem at Pollensa Bay," Mr. Parker Pyne was called upon to play matchmaker. On what island in the Mediterranean Sea was he vacationing?

6. The Hercule Poirot mystery "Yellow Iris" was rewritten into a full-length novel. What was the name of this novel?

7. Which clue led Miss Marple to discover the murderer in "Miss Marple Tells a Story"?

8. At what time did Benedict Farley dream he was going to die in "The Dream"?

9. In the short story "In a Glass Darkly," to whom did Sylvia turn in time of need?

10. Where was Hercule Poirot vacationing when he became involved in the murder in "Problem at Sea"?

## Quiz 47: *The Tuesday Club Murders*

*The Tuesday Club Murders* is a collection of thirteen short stories featuring Miss Marple. The Tuesday Club originated from a dinner party at Miss Marple's home. The conversation turned to unsolved mysteries and the group decided to meet every Tuesday, with each member responsible for telling a story for the others to solve. Each story reminded Miss Marple of a village parallel. Read the synopses and match them with Miss Marple's parallels.

### Stories

1. "The Tuesday Night Club"—Sir Henry Clithering told the tale of a traveling salesman, his wife, and the

wife's companion. All three became ill after the evening meal and Mrs. Jones, the salesman's wife, died. The circumstances were fishy, and Mr. Jones was suspected of murdering his wife.

2. "The Idol House of Astarte"—Dr. Pender told the story of a mysterious murder that took place at a costume party in a haunted summerhouse. Several people watched as a man was murdered, but no one saw the deadly knife until it was found in the body. Was the man murdered by a ghost, or was there an earthly explanation?

3. "Ingots of Gold"—Raymond West told a story about a mysterious adventure he had with his friend. The story involved searching for the *Otranto's* sunken treasure of gold bullion, lost six months earlier off the coast of Cornwall. Raymond's desire for adventure and his credulous temperament led him to witness clandestine racketeering activities. He wasn't sure if his friend was a harmless adventurer or a notorious smuggler.

4. "The Bloodstained Pavement"—Joyce Lempriere, Raymond's future wife, told the story of a time when she was staying in a small inn on the coast of Cornwall. She watched the interchange between a man, his wife, and the man's female friend from his past. All did not seem up to snuff, and sure enough, a few days later the wife was found drowned. Was this a story of conspiracy to get rid of the wife so the man could take up with his old love, or was it just a case of a weak swimmer and a strong current?

5. "Motive vs. Opportunity"—Mr. Petherick, a solicitor, told the story of a client, Simon Clodes, who never got

over the death of his beloved granddaughter. Mr. Clodes turned to a spiritual medium, Mrs. Spragg, and through séances with her, he was able to contact his dead granddaughter. His joy and the influence of Mrs. Spragg led him to disinherit his relatives and leave his money to her, but his new will disappeared. Was this a case of sleight of hand, or did the spirit world intervene over the evil psychic?

6. "The Thumb Mark of St. Peter"—Miss Marple told the story of her niece Mabel, who was recently widowed. The husband was a tyrant and his death was more of a relief than a loss. However, village tongues started wagging after it was disclosed that Mabel had purchased arsenic shortly before her husband's death. She pleaded with Miss Marple for help in sorting things out. To quiet the rumors, the body was exhumed. Was this a case of a desperate wife freeing herself from a violent husband, or was it a frame-up to avenge his death?

7. "The Blue Geranium"—Sir Henry Clithering entertained the group with the tale of a demanding invalid, Mrs. Pritchard. A spiritualist predicted that Mrs. Pritchard would die when the geraniums on her wallpaper turned blue. The prediction came true. Was the power of suggestion too strong for Mrs. Pritchard, or did one of the many characters who benefited from her death take advantage of an excellent opportunity?

8. "The Companion"—Dr. Lloyd told the story of two English ladies vacationing in the Canary Islands. Mrs. Durrant drowned while swimming, but a witness swore that Mrs. Barton intentionally held her companion's head under water. Why would a rich em-

ployer kill her humble companion? Wouldn't it be the
other way around? Maybe it was...

9. "The Four Suspects"—Sir Henry told of a retired
counterspy whose past caught up with him. After he
was killed the four suspects—his devoted niece, his
maid of many years, a local gardener, and a Scotland
Yard–appointed secretary—all seemed to be above
suspicion. Was the murderer an outside hit man with
an excellent cover, or could the victim's death have
nothing to do with his past?

10. "A Christmas Tragedy"—Miss Marple told a story
from her past. She suspected that her friend, Mrs.
Sanders, might have been murdered by her husband.
Miss Marple couldn't figure out, at first, how the
husband had pulled it off. His alibi seemed airtight.
However, he should have found a hat that fitted him,
especially with the eagle eye of Miss Marple looking
on.

11. "The Herb of Death"—It was Dolly Bantry's turn to
tell a story, but she was not good with words. Sir
Henry came to her rescue and suggested a few rounds
of twenty questions to help Mrs. B. with the flow. This
was a case of foxglove poisoning when the dinner
ducks were stuffed with the deadly mistaken-for-sage
herb. Sylvia Keene was the only one to die. Was this a
perfect crime, or was she merely the unintended
victim?

12. "The Affair at the Bungalow"—Jane Heiler, a beautiful, bubbleheaded actress, told of a naive young
playwright who was accused of robbery. He was lured
to the scene of the crime by a woman he mistook for

Miss Heiler. Was he merely at the wrong place at the wrong time, or was he more clever than he looked?

13. "Death by Drowning"—The last case was very close to home. The murder of Rose Emmot took place in St. Mary Mead. Rex Sandford, the father of the victim's unborn child, was the principal suspect. Miss Marple knew immediately who the murderer was and wrote the name down on a piece of paper. She gave the paper to Sir Henry and persuaded him to become involved in the investigation. As it turned out, Miss Marple was right again. How did she do it?

## Miss Marple's village parallels

a. Poor Annie Poultny—She was suspected of making away with old Miss Lamb's will. Annie served Miss Lamb faithfully for over fifty years, and the accusation broke her heart. After Annie died, the will was discovered in a secret drawer where it had been hidden by the absentminded Miss Lamb.

b. Mr. Peasegood, the vegetable peddler—When he sold carrots to Miss Marple's niece, he inadvertently delivered turnips instead.

c. An unconscious man—The poor man was knocked unconscious at Lady Sharpley's garden party. He was arranging the golf clock and tripped over one of the numbers.

d. A district nurse—Miss Marple remembered the time there was some trouble in St Mary Mead with a district nurse. Miss Marple did not go into detail about the incident. She did describe the tendency of nurses to become too involved with the family for whom they worked. After all, nurses are human beings.

e. Mr. Badger, the chemist—He had a whole slew of relatives waiting in line to inherit, and as you would know, his young-enough-to-be-his-daughter housekeeper was really his wife. After Mr. Badger died, his relatives had to stand in a much longer line.

f. Tommy Symonds, a naughty little boy—He tricked his Sunday school teacher, Mrs. Durston, into answering a loaded question: "Do you say yolk of eggs is white or yolk of eggs are white?" Mrs. Durston answered, "Yolks of eggs are white and yolk of egg is white." "Well," Tommy said, "I should say yolk of egg is yellow."

g. Walter Hones—He claimed his wife fell into the river while they were walking home one evening. Miss Marple knew better, but she had no proof.

h. Old Mr. Hargraves—Unbeknownst to his wife, Mr. Hargraves had been living a double life. His other family consisted of his ex-housekeeper and their five children. When he died, the deception was revealed. He left all his money to his illegitimate family, instead of to Mrs. Hargraves.

i. Farmers in Grey Wethers—Things were often taken out of context. For instance, if you were talking to a farmer and mentioned gray weathers he would think you were talking of stone circles instead of meteorology.

j. Mrs. Pebmarsh—She was a laundress who stole an opal pin that was fastened to a customer's blouse. She calculatedly placed it in another woman's blouse.

k. Gardeners—This case was easy to solve. The gardener's story was a lie. Everybody knew that gardeners didn't work on Whit Monday.

l. Mrs. Trout—She had been a companion to several elderly ladies. She managed to draw the old-age pensions of three of those women after they had died. After all, one old woman was just like any other old woman.

m. Mrs. Green—People in St. Mary Mead began to get suspicious when she buried five children and collected life insurance on each of them.

## Quiz 48: *The Under Dog and Other Stories*

*The Under Dog and Other Stories* is a collection of nine short stories featuring Hercule Poirot, Captain Hastings, and Inspector Japp.

1. Who assisted Hercule Poirot in the investigation in "The Under Dog"?
   a. Captain Hastings
   b. Ariadne Oliver
   c. His valet, George
   d. Colonel Race

2. In "The Under Dog," what method did Hercule Poirot use to get Lady Astwell to admit why she suspected Mr. Trefusis?
   a. Word association
   b. Hypnosis
   c. Truth serum
   d. A lie detector

3. "The Plymouth Express" was developed into a novel in 1928. What was the name of the novel?
   a. Murder on the Orient Express
   b. 4:50 from Paddington
   c. Destination Unknown
   d. The Mystery of the Blue Train

4. "The Market Basing Mystery" shared the same plot as another short story from *Dead Man's Mirror*. What was the name of this short story?
   a. "Murder in the Mews"
   b. "Dead Man's Mirror"
   c. "Triangle at Rhodes"
   d. "The Incredible Theft"

5. What was the family curse in "The Lemesurier Inheritance"?
   a. The firstborn son will never have an heir.
   b. The firstborn son will bring disgrace to the family.
   c. The firstborn son will succumb to insanity.
   d. The firstborn son will not live to inherit.

6. Which two short stories in this collection were adapted for the 1989 British TV series, *Agatha Christie's Poirot*, starring David Suchet?
   a. "The Plymouth Express" and "The Under Dog"
   b. "The Adventure of Clapham Cook" and "The King of Clubs"
   c. "The Submarine Plans" and "The Market Basing Mystery"
   d. "The Cornish Mystery" and "The Lemesurier Inheritance"

7. Which short story was reworked to become "The Incredible Theft" in the collection entitled *Dead Man's Mirror?*
   a. "The Submarine Plans"
   b. "The King of Clubs"
   c. "The Affair at the Victory Ball"
   d. "The Cornish Mystery"

8. The harlequin character from "The Affair at the Victory Ball" evolved into the protagonist in another collection of short stories. What was the name of this protagonist?
   a. Hercule Poirot
   b. Inspector Japp
   c. Mr. Quin
   d. Parker Pyne

9. In which short story did Hercule Poirot trade a signed confession for giving the criminal a twenty-four-hour head start on the police?
   a. "The Market Basing Mystery"
   b. "The Cornish Mystery"
   c. "The Adventure of Clapham Cook"
   d. "The Lemesurier Inheritance"

10. Which village was used as the location of *The Seven Dials Mystery* and *Poirot Loses a Client*, and also was the title of its own mystery in this short story collection?
    a. "The Cornish Mystery"
    b. "The Adventure of Clapham Cook"
    c. "The Market Basing Mystery"
    d. "The Lemesurier Inheritance"

# Quiz 49: *Three Blind Mice and Other Stories*

*Three Blind Mice and Other Stories* is a collection of eight short stories and the novella, "Three Blind Mice." It was published in America in 1950. The following quiz contains ten multiple-choice questions.

1. Where did the novella "The Three Blind Mice" have its beginning?
   a. As a short story with the same title
   b. As the stage play *Mousetrap*
   c. As a radio play
   d. As a full-length novel

2. Who received "Three Blind Mice," written in 1947, as a birthday present?
   a. Christie's husband, Max Mallowan
   b. Christie's daughter, Rosalind
   c. Christie's grandson, Mathew
   d. Queen Mary, mother of King George VI

3. In "Strange Jest," what relative of Miss Marple helped her solve the case of the missing fortune?
   a. Miss Marple's grandmother
   b. Miss Marple's uncle Henry
   c. Miss Marple's mother
   d. Miss Marple's nephew Robert

4. What made Miss Marple suspicious of Miss Emily Skinner in "The Case of the Perfect Maid"?
   a. Miss Emily's fake accent
   b. Miss Emily's knowledge of poisons
   c. Miss Emily's refusal to see a doctor even though she was a hypochondriac
   d. Miss Emily's firing of her maid, a local woman

5. What lifted Miss Marple's spirits after a bad case of the flu in "The Case of the Caretaker"?
   a. A murder at Old Hall
   b. A suspicious-looking couple who moved in next door
   c. The disappearance of the vicar's housekeeper
   d. The apparent riding accident of a rich, young wife

6. Whose antics reminded Miss Marple of the murder of Mrs. Spenlow in "The Tape-Measure Murder"?
   a. Miss Marple's two cousins, Antony and Gordon
   b. Miss Marple's aunt and uncle, who took her to Bertram's Hotel
   c. Miss Price and Miss Hartnell, two village spinsters
   d. Tommy Symonds, the village prankster

7. In "The Third-Floor Flat," who was living in the apartment building under an alias of Mr. Connor?
   a. Mr. Quin
   b. Mr. Parker Pyne
   c. Hercule Poirot
   d. Tommy Beresford

8. How did Hercule Poirot assist the Waverlys in "The Adventure of Johnny Waverly"?
   a. Poirot helped Mrs. Waverly locate her biological mother.
   b. Poirot located Mr. Waverly's runaway sister.
   c. Poirot located the Waverly's kidnapped son.
   d. Poirot discovered the true identity of the man claiming to be a long-lost cousin.

9. In "Four and Twenty Blackbirds," what clue put Hercule Poirot on the right track to proving the victim's death was not accidental?
   a. The time the victim dined at Gallant Endeavor

b. The victim's identical twin

c. The letter found in the pocket of the victim's dressing-gown

d. The victim's white, well-brushed teeth

10. The plot of "The Love Detectives" was woven around two people confessing to the same murder. Which Miss Marple mystery had the same characteristic?

a. *The Murder at the Vicarage*

b. *At Bertram's Hotel*

c. *A Caribbean Mystery*

d. *The Body in the Library*

# 6

# The Curtain Rises

The longest-running play in theatrical history celebrates its forty-fourth anniversary on November 25, 1996. *The Mousetrap* has been translated into twenty-two languages, performed in forty-one countries, and witnessed by over four and a half million people. What makes this play so popular? Somewhat baffled by its success, the author herself stated: "Apart from replying with the obvious answer, 'Luck!—because it is luck, ninety percent luck, at least, I should say—the only reason I can give is that there is a bit of something in it for almost everybody: people of different age groups and tastes can enjoy seeing it."

Although Agatha Christie wrote fewer than a dozen original plays, many of her novels and short stories were adapted for the stage. Just as with her novels, Christie adds unforeseen clues and concludes the dramas with the most unexpected endings.

The stage is set in chapter six for you to master the following seven quizzes. The curtain rises.

## Quiz 50: Stage Craft

There are twenty-one plays written by Christie or adapted from her works. Now answer twenty short-answer questions about their stagings and productions.

1. At which theater did *The Mousetrap* open in London in 1952?

2. In which play adaptation did Christie delete Hercule Poirot because she felt that he ruined the book version of the story?

3. What was the name of Agatha Christie's first original play?

4. What play was originally entitled *Clarissa Finds a Body?*

5. In which play adaptation did playwright Michael Morton want to change Hercule Poirot's name to Beau Poirot and make him twenty years younger?

6. Which original play was set in a hospital ward?

7. What mystery did Christie's daughter warn her against adapting for the stage?

8. What play entitled after Act III, Scene 2 of Shakespeare's *Hamlet* was suggested by Christie's son-in-law?

9. According to Christie, what play made her an author as well as a playwright?

10. What was the name of Christie's last play, written when she was eighty years old?

11. What was the title of the collection of Christie's three one-act plays?

12. Agatha Christie refused to give her consent for the production of this play unless she was allowed to change her original ending. What was the title of the play?

13. Which play did Christie first entitle *No Fields of Amaranth?*

14. Which play was never staged, even though it was described by Christie's husband, Max, as being "Agatha's most beautiful and profound play"?

15. Which play did Christie write for British actress Margaret Lockwood?

16. Which play was set in South Wales?

17. Which play featuring Miss Marple was adapted from a mystery of the same title? Clue: It ran for 1,176 performances.

18. What was the name of the play that was a failure on stage, but became a hit at the box office more than twenty years later? Clue: It was adapted from a book with a different title.

19. Which play, produced in America with a more politically correct title, was more successful in New York than in London?

20. What was the name of the play that received a lukewarm reception on its first tour, was rewritten with a similar title, and failed again when it reopened in the West End?

## Quiz 51: Play Adaptations

Five Agatha Christie mysteries were adapted for the stage under a different title. Match each mystery with its stage adaptation in this quiz.

1. *Death on the Nile*
2. *Five Little Pigs*
3. *The Murder of Roger Ackroyd*
4. "Philomel Cottage"
5. *Death Comes as the End*

a. *Alibi*
b. *Love From a Stranger*
c. *Go Back for Murder*
d. *Akhnaton*
e. *Hidden Horizon*

## Quiz 52: *The Mousetrap*

Match the character with Christie's character description in this ten-question quiz.

1. Paravicini
2. Mollie Ralston
3. Major Metcalf
4. Miss Casewell
5. Murder suspect
6. Mrs. Maureen Lyon
7. Sergeant Trotter
8. Mrs. Boyle
9. Giles Ralston
10. Christopher Wren

a. "Medium height, wearing darkish overcoat, lightish scarf, and soft felt hat."
b. "...is a cheerful, commonplace young man with a slight cockney accent.
c. He is a rather wild-looking neurotic young man."

d. "He is foreign and dark and elderly with a flamboyant moustache."

e. "She is a large, imposing woman in a very bad temper."

f. "He is a rather arrogant but attractive young man in his twenties."

g. "...a middle-aged, square-shouldered man, very military in manner and bearing."

h. "She is a young woman of a manly type and carries a case."

i. "She is a tall, pretty young woman with an ingenuous air, in her twenties.

j. The murdered woman

## Quiz 53: *Verdict*

Here are ten statements about the plot of *Verdict*. Answer whether each statement is true or false.

1. Anya was bitter toward her husband, Karl Hendryk, because he was healthy and she was an invalid.

2. When Lester stole Professor Hendryk's rare book and sold it for money to take a girl on a date, the Professor refused to continue tutoring Lester.

3. Sir William Rollander was unable to convince Karl Hendryk to tutor Rollander's daughter.

4. Lisa Koletzky, hired to take care of Anya, was a physicist by profession.

5. Helen Rollander, Sir William's daughter, boasted to Karl Hendryk that she murdered Hendryk's wife.

6. Karl Hendryk was unable to get Helen to confess to the murder because she left town immediately when she realized that Professor Hendryk was not in love with her.

7. Lisa Koletzky was arrested for the murder of Anya Hendryk.

8. The shock of the murder caused Professor Hendryk to realize that he really did love his wife.

9. The play received rave reviews on opening night.

10. Agatha Christie considered the play one of her weakest scripts and would have been happier with the original ending.

## Quiz 54: *Black Coffee*

This quiz contains ten statements about the plot, characters, and production of the theatrical thriller *Black Coffee*. Answer either true or false to each statement.

1. Sir Claud Amory's son, Richard, left the army voluntarily to assist his father with his scientific experiments.

2. Sir Claud was murdered by someone trying to steal his formula for a new explosive, Amorite.

3. Sir Claud knew the thief was among the members of his own household. He gathered everyone together and announced that if the thief did not return the formula by noon, he would change his will and disinherit everyone.

4. Thinking that the formula had been returned, Richard Amory dismissed Poirot. However, Sir Claud's sister, Caroline, suspected foul play in her brother's death and requested that Poirot stay involved.

5. Thinking she was alone, Richard's wife, Lucia, poured poisonous tablets into her hand. But Raynor, the secretary, observed Lucia's actions from the doorway.

6. Lucia Amory was really Selma Goetz, an international spy who was believed to be dead.

7. Captain Hastings became infatuated with one of the murder suspects, Sir Claud's niece, Barbara.

8. Inspector Battle investigated the murder.

9. Agatha Christie's agent did not approve of the play and suggested that she forget it entirely.

10. Agatha did not attend the opening of this play because she was ill with influenza.

## Quiz 55: *Spider's Web*

Quiz fifty-five contains ten statements about the plot, characters, and the original production of *Spider's Web*. Answer true or false to each statement.

1. The play opened with Sir Rowland "Roly" Delahaye and Hugh Birch competing in a taste-test to distinguish three different glasses of port. Hugh Birch won the contest.

2. Oliver Costello went to Copplestone Court to convince Henry Hailsham-Brown and his new wife, Clarissa, that Pippa should live with Costello and Pippa's mother, Miranda, who was Costello's wife.

3. Clarissa wanted to dispose of Oliver Costello's dead body because she thought her stepdaughter, Pippa, had killed him.

4. Clarissa attempted to give Roly, Hugh, Jeremy, and herself an alibi by setting up a game of bridge reflecting the scores of two rubbers.

5. Inspector Lord saw through Clarissa's alibi when he discovered the ace of spades under the sofa.

6. The message that appeared in two places, the secret compartment and the hidden panel, was "Sucks to you!"

7. Clarissa's second attempt to hide Costello's body from the police was successful.

8. Clarissa caught the killer just as he was about to strike again and kill Pippa.

9. Peter Saunders, producer of several Christie plays, suggested that she turn *Spider's Web* into a comedy.

10. The play only ran for five months, probably because two other Christie plays were running at the same time.

## Quiz 56: *The Unexpected Guest*

The following ten statements are about the plot, characters, and production of *The Unexpected Guest*. Answer true or false to each statement.

1. Michael Starkwedder, a stranger, said he was in the neighborhood on the night of the murder because he was looking for old landmarks of the area where his mother used to live.

2. The murder victim, Richard Warwick, was crippled when he was mauled by a lion while on safari in Kenya.

3. Two people confessed to the murder of Richard Warwick.

4. Richard Warwick drank in order to deal with the guilt of having run over and killed a child while he was under the influence of alcohol.

5. Jan Warwick, Richard's half brother, was afraid of Richard because he threatened to have Jan committed.

6. Henry Angell, Richard's nurse, threatened to black-mail Laura Warwick with damaging information about the murder that Angell had withheld from the police.

7. Inspector Thomas discovered that Major Julian Farrar was in Richard's study on the night of the murder when Thomas found Farrar's fingerprints on Warwick's desk.

8. Laura Warwick saw the true colors of her lover, Julian Farrar, when he would not support her emotionally because he thought she might be the murderer.

9. The murderer shot Jan Warwick to silence him.

10. *The Unexpected Guest*, which opened at London's Duchess Theatre in 1958, ran for only fourteen performances.

# 7

# Lights, Camera, Action!

The credits read like a *Who's Who* of British and American actors. Bette Davis, Basil Rathbone, Rock Hudson, Olivia de Havilland, Helen Hayes, David Niven, and Marlene Dietrich are just a few of the names from a long list of prestigious actors who have starred in the many films since 1928 that were based on Agatha Christie's works. We've even come to recognize Academy Award winner Margaret Rutherford as the lovable Miss Marple. The character of Hercule Poirot has been portrayed by such greats as Charles Laughton, as the first Poirot, and Peter Ustinov, Albert Finney, and James Coco. Academy Award winners Dustin Hoffman and Vanessa Redgrave appeared in *Agatha*, a semibiographical film about her mysterious disappearance in 1926.

Many of Christie's books have been adapted to the silver screen more than once. In some cases, the screenplays adopted different endings. Each time the stories were as compelling as the author's original endings.

John Brabourne and Richard Goodwin produced the two most successful Christie films, *Death on the Nile* and *Murder on the Orient Express*. Christie's mysteries have been made into more than twenty-eight movies and over a dozen are available on videos. These movies have become cult classics and the videos command their own Agatha Christie section in many stores.

Chapter seven contains three quizzes regarding movie and television adaptations of Christie's mysteries. Quiet on the set!

## Quiz 57: Behind the Scenes

This quiz contains twenty-five multiple choice questions concerning interesting bits of information surrounding the movie and television productions of Christie's works.

1. After this movie's New York opening, its distribution was postponed for two months and rescheduled for just when the King Tut exhibit opened.
   a. *Murder on the Orient Express*
   b. *Death on the Nile*
   c. *The Mirror Crack'd*
   d. *Appointment With Death*
   e. *Evil Under the Sun*

2. Each day around noon when *Death on the Nile* was filmed, there was a two-hour delay because
   a. The sand fleas were intolerable at that time of the day.
   b. A local religious custom required that no work be done during that time.
   c. The sun was too bright for filming.
   d. Too many tourists were out and about.
   e. The temperature usually soared to around 130 degrees.

3. Which actor in the role of Hercule Poirot disappointed Agatha Christie because his moustache was not up to par?
   a. Albert Finney, in *Murder an the Orient Express*
   b. Peter Ustinov, in *Evil Under the Sun*
   c. Tony Randall, in *The Alphabet Murders*
   d. Austin Trevor, in *Lord Edgware Dies*
   e. David Suchet, in *Agatha Christie's Poirot*

4. At the 1974 Academy Awards, which movie edged out *Murder on the Orient Express* for Best Screenplay Adapted from Other Material?
   a. *Apprenticeship of Duddy Kravitz*
   b. *The Godfather, Part II*
   c. *Lenny*
   d. *Young Frankenstein*
   e. *Chinatown*

5. Which film adaptation was one of Agatha Christie's favorites but was a failure at the box office?
   a. *Endless Night*
   b. *Love From a Stranger*
   c. *Appointment With Death*
   d. *Ordeal by Innocence*
   e. *Murder Ahoy!*

6. Which actress did Christie dislike in the role of Miss Marple
   a. Angela Lansbury
   b. Helen Hayes
   c. Margaret Rutherford
   d. Joan Hickson
   e. Gracie Fields

7. Which actress wore a pair of reptile shoes made from twenty-six python skins in the movie *Death on the Nile?*
   a. Bette Davis
   b. Mia Farrow
   c. Angela Lansbury
   d. Lois Chiles
   e. Olivia Hussey

8. Which Agatha Christie film netted the most revenue?
   a. *Witness for the Prosecution*
   b. *Ordeal by Innocence*
   c. *Ten Little Indians*
   d. *Death on the Nile*
   e. *Murder on the Orient Express*

9. Which movie production was initially abandoned because Christie was not pleased with the adaptation's bedroom scene involving Poirot?
   a. *Murder on the Orient Express*
   b. *Evil Under the Sun*
   c. *Appointment With Death*
   d. *The Alphabet Murders*
   e. *Death on the Nile*

10. Which actor played Poirot in seven films?
    a. David Suchet
    b. Tony Randall
    c. Albert Finney
    d. Austin Trevor
    e. Peter Ustinov

11. In *Murder With Mirrors*, which actor/actress was recovering from a stroke at the time of filming?
    a. Helen Hayes
    b. John Mills
    c. Bette Davis
    d. Leo McKern
    e. Dorothy Tutin

12. How many times was the mystery *Ten Little Indians* made into a movie?
    a. Four
    b. Three
    c. Two
    d. One
    e. Five

13. What was the first Agatha Christie mystery adapted for the screen?
    a. *Adventure, Inc.*
    b. *Alibi*
    c. *Lord Edgware Dies*
    d. *Black Coffee*
    e. *Love From a Stranger*

14. Which Hollywood actor, unsure of his ability to play a man with a heart condition, faked a heart attack at home in preparation for his performance in *Witness for the Prosecution*?
    a. Beau Bridges
    b. David Horne
    c. Francis L. Sullivan
    d. Charles Laughton
    e. Tyrone Power

15. Which Christie movie received six Academy Award nominations, but did not win an Oscar?
    a. *Death on the Nile*
    b. *Appointment With Death*
    c. *Witness for the Prosecution*
    d. *Murder on the Orient Express*
    e. *Evil Under the Sun*

16. Which actress played Miss Marple more times than anyone else?
    a. Margaret Rutherford
    b. Angela Lansbury
    c. Joan Hickson
    d. Helen Hayes
    e. Gracie Fields

17. Whose voice was that of Mr. Owen in the 1975 version of *Ten Little Indians?*
    a. James Mason's
    b. Peter Lorre's
    c. Richard Attenborough's
    d. John Huston's
    e. Orson Welles's

1 8. What authentic props were used in the screen version of *Murder on the Orient Express?*
    a. The real Orient Express cars
    b. The costumes, which came from a vintage clothing museum
    c. The furnishings for the coaches, which were antiques from the 1930s
    d. Actual menus often used on the Orient Express
    e. The Orient Express bar and its furnishings

19. What gala premiere of an Agatha Christie film did Queen Elizabeth attend?
   a. *Witness for the Prosecution*
   b. *Death on the Nile*
   c. *Ten Little Indians*
   d. *Murder on the Orient Express*
   e. *The Alphabet Murders*

20. Margaret Rutherford and Joan Hickson both appeared in which Miss Marple film?
   a. *Murder at the Gallop*
   b. *Body in the Library*
   c. *Murder Ahoy!*
   d. *Murder She Said*
   e. *At Bertram's Hotel*

21. Which film version of *Funerals Are Fatal*, starring Margaret Rutherford, substituted Miss Marple for Hercule Poirot as the story's sleuth?
   a. *Murder Most Foul*
   b. *Murder at the Gallop*
   c. *Murder Ahoy!*
   d. *Murder She Said*
   e. *4:50 from Paddington*

22. Which mystery was filmed three times, each time with a different setting?
   a. *The A.B.C. Murders*
   b. *The Mirror Crack'd*
   c. *Ordeal by Innocence*
   d. *Appointment With Death*
   e. *Ten Little Indians*

23. Which film won three out of seven British Film Awards, received six Academy Award nominations, and won the Oscar for Best Supporting Actress?

a. *Murder on the Orient Express*
b. *Witness for the Prosecution*
c. *Murder with Mirrors*
d. *Death on the Nile*
e. *Lord Edgware Dies*

24. Who won the Oscar for Best Supporting Actress in the film that was the answer to the preceding question?
    a. Ingrid Bergman
    b. Lauren Bacall
    c. Helen Hayes
    d. Elizabeth Taylor
    e. Maggie Smith

25. For which Christie film did Dave Brubeck write the score and perform the music?
    a. *Evil Under the Sun*
    b. *Appointment With Death*
    c. *The Mirror Crack'd*
    d. *Ordeal by Innocence*
    e. *Death on the Nile*

## Quiz 58: Casting Calls

In this quiz, match the actors or actresses with the Agatha Christie characters they portrayed in movie or television adaptations of her works. This is a fifty-question quiz. The year each adaptation was made is noted.

1. Hercule Poirot in *Alibi* (1931)
2. George Lovell in *Love from a Stranger* (1937)
3. Carol Howard in *Love from a Stranger* (1937)

a. Piper Laurie
b. Jenny Seagrove
c. David Suchet
d. Peter Ustinov
e. Richard Attenborough

4. The Judge in *Ten Little Indians* (1945)
5. Tommy Beresford in *The Case of the Missing Lady* (early 1950s)
6. Tuppence Beresford in *The Case of the Missing Lady* (early 1950s)
7. Letitia Blacklock in *A Murder Is Announced* (1956)
8. Miss Jane Marple in *A Murder Is Announced* (1956)
9. Patrick Simmons in *A Murder Is Announced* (1956)
10. Leonard Vole in *Witness for the Prosecution* (1957)
11. Christine Vole in *Witness for the Prosecution* (1957)
12. Sir Wilfrid Robarts in *Witness for the Prosecution* (1957)
13. Captain deCourcy Rhumstone in *Murder Ahoy!* (1964)
14. Miss Jane Marple in *Murder Most Foul* (1964)
15. Hugh Lombard in *Ten Little Indians* (1965)
16. Mike Raven in *Ten Little Indians* (1965)

f. Beau Bridges
g. Donald Sutherland
h. Mia Farrow
i. Albert Finney
j. Christopher Plummer
k. Fabian
l. Jean Stapleton
m. Basil Rathbone
n. Tony Randall
o. Cloris Leachman
p. Bette Davis
q. Hayley Mills
r. Barry Fitzgerald
s. Hugh O'Brian
t. Austin Trevor
u. Charles Laughton
v. Stephanie Zimbalist
w. Jonathan Cecil
x. Tyrone Power
y. Geraldine Chaplin
z. Bill Bixby
aa. Marlene Dietrich
bb. Rock Hudson
cc. Deborah Kerr
dd. Sir John Gielgud
ee. Ronald Reagan
ff. Lauren Bacall
gg. Diana Rigg
hh. Joan Hickson
ii. Cheryl Campbell
jj. Jessica Tandy
kk. Gracie Fields
ll. Roger Moore
mm. Jacqueline Bisset
nn. Lionel Jeffries

17. Hercule Poirot in *The Alphabet Murders* (1965)
18. Ellie Rogers in *Endless Night* (1972)
19. Countess Andrenyi in *Murder on the Orient Express* (1974)
20. Hercule Poirot in *Murder on the Orient Express* (1974)
21. Judge Cannon in *Ten Little Indians* (1975)
22. Jacqueline de Bellefort in *Death on the Nile* (1978)
23. Miss Van Schuyler in *Death on the Nile* (1978)
24. Marina Rudd in *The Mirror Crack'd* (1980)
25. Jason Rudd in *The Mirror Crack'd* (1980)
26. Miss Jane Marple in *The Mirror Crack'd* (1980)
27. Ella Zielinsky in *The Mirror Crack'd* (1980)
28. Marquis of Caterham in *The Seven Dials Mystery* (1981)
29. Lady Eileen Brent in *The Seven Dials Mystery* (1981)
30. Daphne Castle in *Evil Under the Sun* (1982)

oo. Olivia de Havilland
pp. Faye Dunaway
qq. Roddy McDowall
rr. Elizabeth Taylor
ss. Margaret Rutherford
tt. Angela Lansbury
uu. James Mason
vv. Helen Hayes
ww. Ann Harding
xx. Maggie Smith

31. Odell Gardener in *Evil Under the Sun* (1982)
32. Rex Brewster in *Evil Under the Sun* (1982)
33. Leonard Vole in *Witness for the Prosecution* (1982)
34. Romaine in *Witness for the Prosecution* (1982)
35. Nurse Plimsoll in *Witness for the Prosecution* (1982)
36. Honoria Waynflete in *Murder Is Easy* (1982)
37. Luke Williams in *Murder Is Easy* (1982)
38. Miss Jane Marple in *A Caribbean Mystery* (1983)
39. Dr. Arthur Calgary in *Ordeal by Innocence* (1985)
40. Rachel Argyle in *Ordeal by Innocence* (1985)
41. Leo Argyle in *Ordeal by Innocence* (1985)
42. Mrs. Ariadne Oliver in *Dead Man's Folly* (1986)
43. Arthur Hastings in *Murder in Three Acts* (1986)
44. Miss Jane Marple in *At Bertram's Hotel* (1987)
45. Emily Boyton in *Appointment With Death* (1988)
46. Lady Westholme in *Appointment With Death* (1988)
47. Hercule Poirot in *Appointment With Death* (1988)
48. Dr. Sarah King in *Appointment With Death* (1988)
49. Anne Beddingfeld in *The Man in the Brown Suit* (1989)
50. Hercule Poirot in *Agatha Christie's Poirot* series (1989)

## Quiz 59: *Agatha*, the Movie

The following questions are about the semibiographical movie *Agatha*, which was produced in 1977, the year following Agatha Christie's death.

1. Who played Agatha in the movie?

2. Who played her husband, Colonel Archibald Christie?

3. Who played the American journalist, Wally Stanton?

4. Which new film company produced the movie? Clue: It was created by several Americans actors in an attempt to compete with the major studios.

5. Who wrote the novel *Agatha*, upon which the movie was based?

6. Who directed the movie?

7. Who was the executive producer?

8. Who wrote the screenplay?

9. Why did Agatha Christie, Ltd. file for an injunction to halt production of the film?

10. Who was hired by the production company to oversee all its business? Clue: He eventually took control of the production of *Agatha*, in spite of a second lawsuit filed by the company's own executive producer.

# 8

# Agatha Christie's Life and Times

What started as a dare ended up creating the best-known, most successful mystery writer ever to put pen to paper. Agatha Christie's success surprised even her. "...I had written a detective story; it had been accepted, and was going to appear in print. There, as far as I was concerned, the matter ended. Certainly at that moment I did not envisage writing any more books." Her modesty did not interfere with her confidence, and she went on to create hundreds of masterful stories. Where did this ordinary middle-class English lady get such bizarre ideas to evolve into some of the most incredible mysteries ever written?

Growing up in Devonshire, a seaside resort in Torquay, England, at the close of the nineteenth century, Agatha Mary Clarissa Miller appears to have had a very normal childhood. However, her mother was a bit eccentric and she even seemed to be clairvoyant at times. Together they created fanciful games that may later have led to the development of many of Christie's plots.

This chapter focuses on the life of Agatha Christie. Although her lengthy two-volume autobiography is very factual, how much did the shy, introverted author really reveal about herself? Can you read between the lines?

## Quiz 60: Agatha Mary Clarissa Miller's Life and Times

This quiz contains thirty short-answer questions on Agatha Christie's private life.

1. When was Agatha Christie born?

2. What was the name of Agatha's favorite rocking horse? Clue: she mentions this childhood toy in her last novel, *Postern of Fate*, by giving the horse therein the same name.

3. What was the name of the terrifying character of her recurring nightmares?

4. Who introduced Agatha to the stories of Sherlock Holmes?

5. What were Agatha's parents' names?

6. Agatha's mother suffered from what ailment after the death of her husband?

7. What did Agatha's father do for a living?

8. In what year did Agatha's mother die?

9. What finishing school did Agatha attend in Paris?

10. What fantastic event occurred to her on May 10, 1911?

11. What was the name of the major who proposed to Agatha a few weeks after meeting her at a fancy-dress dance at the Ralston Patricks?

12. Where was her coming out party?

13. Where did Agatha meet Archie Christie?

14. What did Agatha do to occupy her time while Archie was away on military duty?

15. When was Agatha's daughter, Rosalind, born?

16. After her divorce from Archie Christie, where did Agatha and her daughter Rosalind retreat in order to escape the press?

17. When was Agatha made a dame of the British Empire?

18. Who was Agatha's live-in secretary and long-time companion?

19. True or false: Agatha's grandmother inspired her to write her first detective story.

20. True or false: Agatha's first editor was John Lane at The Bodley Head publishing company.

21. True or false: Edward Cork was Agatha's first agent.

22. True or False: Agatha got her idea for the character of Hercule Poirot from her Belgian butler.

23. True or false: *Giant's Bread* was the name of the romance novel Agatha wrote in three days, calling in sick to work in order to finish it.

24. True or false: Agatha initially wanted to publish her books under the pen name of Martin West.

25. True or false: Agatha's inspiration for *Death on the Nile* came from when she spent time in Egypt as a teenager.

26. True or false: Most of her characters were based on real people.

27. What was the date of Agatha's mysterious disappearance?

28. How long was she missing?

29. Where was she during this time?

30. What name did she use and why was this significant?

# 9

# Agatha Christie Crossword Puzzles

As a bonus, here are three Agatha Christie crossword puzzles.

Puzzle one, "Mystery Titles and More," contains forty clues concerning the titles of Agatha Christie's mysteries. Some of the answers are complete titles and some contain a key word from the title. Puzzle two, "British Terms," contains twenty clues of British colloquialisms and formal terms. These words appeared in Christie's works. "Poisons and Toxins," puzzle three, offers the reader the opportunity to identify substances used by Christie's characters to commit murder. This quiz contains thirty clues. Not all the terms are used in Christie's works, but they should be familiar to the reader. Sharpen your pencil and begin.

## Puzzle 1—Mystery Titles & More

### ACROSS

1 Last Hercule Poirot mystery
2 Looking glass
4 In how many acts did the tragedy occur?
6 Comes as the end
8 Used to commit murder
10 "Snoozing" murder

13 The "secret enemy"

15 Christie-type mystery

16 Mallowan's first name

18 Ariadne Oliver received credit for writing *The Body in the Library*—4 words

24 Pocket full of this grain

25 Constable on patrol

27 Mystery that featured Ariadne Oliver alone

28 Christie's one-act play

30 Adjudication

31 Unpopular item at Bertram's hotel

32 Poirot's brother

34 Mystern in which Tuppence was grazed by a bullet in her backyard—3 words

35 Biblical city near Baghdad

## DOWN

1 Tragic holiday

3 Agent of vengeance

4 Meeting night for murder

5 "Old___," central criminal court

6 Christie's dedication of *The Mystery of the Blue Train*

7 Occurred at End House

9 River in Egypt

11 Where was Poirot's first mysterious affair?

12 Ackroyd's first name

13 Lizzy Borden's murder weapon

14 Location of Miss Marple's first murder

16 Who's dead?—2 words

17 Superintendent Battle was assisted by his nephew—2 words

19 Christie's daughter's first name

20 Whose thumbmark?

21 English breakfast

22  Who can remember?
23  Became *Death in the Clouds*
26  Mystery that mentioned Poirot's fictitious brother—3
    words
29  Poison
33  Coach that became the Orient Express

## Puzzle 2—British Terms

**ACROSS**

4 Lawyer who prepares cases for barristers
7 English dish—two words
8 Gazebo
11 Prize in plum pudding—two words
14 British title of honor given to a woman
16 Light afternoon meal

17  Nine iron
19  Lawyer who tries court cases

## DOWN

1  Apartment
2  Smoked or salted fish
3  truck
5  Restroom
6  Secretary (two words)
8  2 weeks
9  Sweet biscuit made with currants
10  English currency
11  Blocks draft under door
12  Elevator
13  Milk punch
15  Tract of swampy wasteland
18. Nightstick

## Puzzle 3—Poisons & Drugs

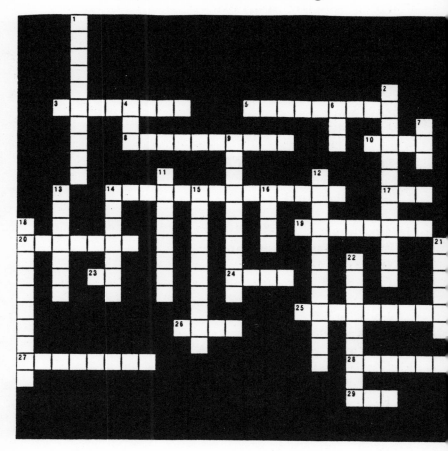

### ACROSS

3 Alkaloid that affects the central nervous system used in *Black Coffee*

5 Drug used by cardiac patients

8 Rat poison used in *The Mysterious Mr. Quin*

10 Substance containing toxic fumes

14  Mickey Finn
17  Poisonous plant that causes irritation to the skin
19  Poisonous leafy plant used in *Postern of Fate*
20  Eye drops used in *Crooked House*
23  Overdose, abbr.
24  Blowgun ammunition
25  Drug that increases the heart rate
26  Tablet
27  Liquid alkaloid that causes respiratory failure
28  "Take two, and call me in the morning."
29  Matter form of hydrogen cyanide in the clocks

## DOWN

1  Knockout drops
2  Drug that causes false reality
4  Central nervous system, abbr.
6  Drug purchased without prescription
7  Color of oceanic poisonous tide caused by microorganism
9  Belladonna
11  Derivative of opium used in *Sad Cypress*
12  Cardiac drug used in *Verdict*
13  Narcotic often found in cough medicine
14  Lingering smell of bitter almonds as in *Endless Night*
15  Fights infections
16  Alloted drug amount
18  Drug that slows down reactions
21  Drug derived from mescal
22  Venom from South American tree snake used in *Death in the Air*

# Part 2

# Answers

# Quiz I: Titles and Plots

1. *Peril at End House*
2. *Murder in Mesopotamia*
3. *The Body in the Library*
4. *Evil Under the Sun*
5. *Thirteen at Dinner*
6. *Easy to Kill*
7. *Poirot Loses a Client*
8. *Murder After Hours*
9. *The Seven Dials Mystery*
10. *Death on the Nile*
11. *N or M?*
12. *The Murder at the Vicarage*
13. *The Big Four*
14. *The Mysterious Affair at Styles*
15. *Cards on the Table*
16. *The Moving Finger*
17. *Murder for Christmas*
18. *Crooked House*
19. *They Came to Baghdad*
20. *Murder on the Orient Express*
21. *Funerals Are Fatal*
22. *Murder with Mirrors*
23. *Dead Man's Folly*
24. *The Murder of Roger Ackroyd*
25. *The A.B.C. Murders*
26. *Towards Zero*
27. *The Boomerang Clue*
28. *The Secret of the Chimneys*
29. *Ten Little Indians*
30. *Ordeal by Innocence*

## Quiz 2: Alternate Titles

1. f. *The Sittaford Mystery*
2. i. *Why Didn't They Ask Evans?*
3. g. *Destination Unknown*
4. o. *An Overdose of Death; x. One, Two, Buckle My Shoe*
5. k. *Mystery at Littlegreen House; n. Dumb Witness*
6. aa. *Murder In the Calais Coach*
7. r. *After the Funeral*
8. z. *Lord Edgware Dies*
9. bb. *Murder Is Easy*
10. h. *Three Act Tragedy*
11. w. *Five Little Pigs*
12. cc. *A Holiday for Murder*
13. e. *The Hollow*
14. a. *Hickory, Dickory, Dock*
15. b. *Death in the Clouds*
16. m. *And Then There Were None*
17. y. *They Do It With Mirrors*
18. v. *Sparkling Cyanide*
19. i. *4:50 From Paddington; t. Murder She Said*
20. c. *The Mirror Crack'd from Side to Side*
21. g. *Come and Be Hanged*
22. j. *Taken at the Flood*
23. p. *Blood Will Tell*
24. d. *Murder in the Mews*
25. s. *Parker Pyne Investigates*

## Quiz 3: Murderers, Motives, and Victims

1. Victim—Samuel Edward Ratchett
2. Motive—Mrs. Badcock exposed Marina Gregg to German measles, causing her child to be born mentally retarded.
3. Victim—Sir Bartholomew Strange

4. Motive—Love and money. Lady Sedgwick's daughter, Elvira Blake, found out that her mother was married to the doorman, Michael Gorman. Therefore, the mother's second marriage to Elvira's father was illegal, and Elvira would not be able to inherit her mother's money. The only way Elivra Blake could keep her greedy lover was with a hefty bank account.

5. Motive—Robbery; the thief was Richard Knighton.

6. Motive—Yahmose's hunger for power grew into a need to kill. His victims included Nofret, Satipy, Ipy, Esa, and Henet.

7. Murderer—Lady Westholme

8. Victim—Gerry Wade

9. Murderer—Letitia Blacklock; Victims and Motives— Rudi Scherz recognized Letitia from the past. Amy Murgatroyd suspected Letitia of staging the crime. Letitia was afraid Dora would reveal Letitia's true identity.

10. Motive—Honoria Waynflete never recovered from losing her family home. However, she was coping until Lord Easterfield jilted her when he became acquainted with her dark side. This was the last straw and she felt he had to be severely punished.

11. Motive—Gerda Christow discovered that her husband had a lover before their marriage. The ex-lover appeared on the scene after many years, and she and Dr. Christow had a moonlit rendezvous. Gerda found out and suspected that her husband was still in love with the other woman. This was too much for sweet Gerda to bear.

12. Motive—Nurse Hopkins convinced Mary to make a will that would allow the nurse to inherit her fortune under an assumed name.

13. Motive—Tim Kendal overheard Major Palgrave telling someone that he recognized Kendal as a murderer.

14. Victims—Ruby Keene and Pamela Reeves. The body in the library was that of Pamela Reeves. Ruby Keene's body was discovered in the wrecked car.

15. Motive—Christian Gulbrandsen discovered that Lewis Serrocold was embezzling the trust funds to gain money to establish an overseas project.

16. Motive—Dr. Quimper wanted to marry the rich Emma Crankenthrope, but his wife did not believe in divorce. He thought that murder would be his route to an easy life.

17. Motive—Ann Shapland killed Miss Springer because the teacher caught her searching for stolen jewels. Mademoiselle Blanche tried to blackmail Shapland, and Shapland also killed her. Miss Vansittart was killed by Miss Chadwick because Miss Vansittart was to take over as head of the school, a position that Miss Chadwick felt belonged to her.

18. Murderer—Norman Gale, a.k.a. James Richards

19. Motive—Garfield wanted money to purchase a Greek island. Murder was his ticket to paradise. His victims were Joyce Reynolds, Mrs. Llewellyn-Smythe, Charlotte Benfield, Lesley Ferrier, Janet White, and Leopold Reynolds.

20. Victims—Mrs. Lancaster believed she was following the command of a higher power. She was instructed to kill young children in atonement for having an abortion when she was seventeen.

## Quiz 4: Aliases

1. Enoch Arden was Charles Trent; Rosaleen Cloads was Eileen Corrigan.
2. Nurse Hopkins was Mary Draper and Mary Riley.
3. Mrs. Blenkensop was Tuppence Beresford.

4. Father Lavigny was Raoul Menier; Dr. Leidner was Frederick Bosner.
5. Mr. Curry was Quentin Duguesclin.
6. Albert Evans was Lance Fortescue.
7. Samuel Edward Ratchett was Cassetti.
8. Dorothea Preston-Grey posed as Lady Margaret Ravenscroft.
9. Ada Mason was really Kitty Kidd.
10. Nigel Chapman was Nigel Stanley.
11. Letitia Blacklock was Charlotte Blacklock.
12. Hilary Craven was Olive Betterton.
13. Caroline Crale was Carla Lemarchant.
14. Walter Drake was Monkey Coleman
15. Sir James Peel Edgerton was known as Mr. Brown.
16. Andrew Restarick was Robert Orwell; Mary Restarick was Frances Cary.
17. Sir George Stubbs was James Folliat.
18. Paul Renauld was George Conneau.
19. Stephen Farr was Stephen Grant, Simeon Lee's son; Pilar Estravados was Conchita Lopez.
20. Mrs. Albert Chapman and Helen Montressor were both portrayed by Gerda Grant, a talented actress.

## Quiz 5: Murder Settings

1. *At Bertram's Hotel*
2. *Appointment With Death*
3. *Endless Night*
4. *The Secret Adversary*
5. *The Patriotic Murders*
6. *Evil Under the Sun*
7. *Nemesis*
8. *Peril at End Hosue*
9. *Elephants Can Remember*

10. *Poirot Loses a Client*
11. *Curtain*
12. *The Man in the Brown Suit*
13. *Murder in Three Acts*
14. *The ABC Murders*
15. *Towards Zero*
16. *There Is a Tide*
17. *Mrs. McGinty's Dead*
18. *The Body in the Library*
19. *Murder in Retrospect*
20. *A Murder Is Announced*

## Quiz 6: Murder Weapons and Victims

1. Small dagger from Tunis
   p. *The Murder of Roger Ackroyd*/Roger Ackroyd
2. Strangled in sleep, victim's face disfigured
   e. *The Mystery of the Blue Train*/Ruth Kettering
3. Green baize tube
   d. *Murder at Hazelmoor*/Captain Trevelyan
4. Kitchen skewer inserted at the base of the skull
   h. *The Moving Finger*/Agnes Woddell
5. Nicotine-laced glass of port
   k. *Murder in Three Acts*/Sir Bartholomew Strange
6. Burned in the fireplace
   c. *The Big Four*/Mr. Paynter
7. Thorn laced with poison
   m. *Death in the Air*/Madame Giselle
8. Hit-and-run
   B. *Easy to Kill*/Miss Mildred Fullerton
9. Cyanide-laced champagne
   j. *Remembered Death*/Rosemary Barton
10. Morphia slipped into a double brandy
    f. *Hickory, Dickory, Death*/Mrs. Nicoletis

11. Taxene in the marmalade
    r. *A Pocket Full of Rye*/Rex Fortescue
12. Knocked on the noggin with a cosh
    a. *The Pale Horse*/Father Gorman
13. Drowned in a bucket of apples
    n. *Hallowe'en Party*/Joyce Reynolds
14. Bashed in the head eight times with a hatchet
    t. *Funerals Are Fatal*/Cora Abernethie Lansquenet
15. Stabbed in the back and buried in a shallow grave on the golf course
    s. *Murder on the Links*/Paul Renauld
16. Strangled by her possessive brother
    o. *Sleeping Murder*/Helen Halliday
17. Stabbed in the heart with a silver fruit knife
    i. *The Clocks*/Mr. Curry
18. Poisoned by a salad mixed with foxglove leaves
    g. *Postern of Fate*/Mary Jordan
19. Cyanide capsules in hay fever medication
    l. *Endless Night*/Ellie (Fenella) Rogers
20. Eserine in the insulin bottle
    Q. *Crooked House*/Aristide Leonides

## Quiz 7: Quotations

1. Esa—*Death Comes as the End*
2. Derek Kettering—*The Mystery of the Blue Train*
3. Inspector Lejeune—*A Pale Horse*
4. Raymond Boynton—*Appointment With Death*
5. Chief Inspector Fred Davy of Scotland Yard—*At Bertram's Hotel*
6. An actor in the play *The Duchess of Malfi*—*Sleeping Murder*
7. Jane Wilkinson—*Thirteen at Dinner*
8. Mrs. Crale—*Murder in Retrospect*

9. Mrs. Burton-Cox—*Elephants Can Remember*
10. Mrs. Lancaster—*By the Pricking of My Thumbs*
11. Hercule Poirot—*A Holiday for Murder*
12. Miss Marple, quoting Tommy Symonds—*The Tuesday Club Murders*
13. Anne Beddingfeld, as narrated by Colonel Race—*The Man in the Brown Suit*
14. Daphne Theodofanous—*Passenger to Frankfurt*
15. Anne Johnson—*Murder in Mesopotamia*

## Quiz 8: First Lines

1. *Postern of Fate*
2. *The Murder at the Vicarage*
3. *Ten Little Indians*
4. *Endless Night*
5. *Murder With Mirrors*
6. *The Pale Horse*
7. *There Is a Tide*
8. *Curtain*
9. *Murder on the Orient Express*
10. *The Boomerang Clue*
11. *So Many Steps to Death*
12. *Funerals Are Fatal*
13. *Ordeal by Innocence*
14. *The Seven Dials Mystery*
15. *Remembered Death*
16. *Thirteen at Dinner*
17. *Murder in Mesopotamia*
18. *Sleeping Murder*
19. *Passenger to Frankfurt*
20. *Elephants Can Remember*

## Quiz 9: Last Words

1. *The Murder of Roger Ackroyd*
2. *Towards Zero*
3. *The Clocks*
4. *The ABC Murders*
5. *Dead Man's Folly*
6. *Death on the Nile*
7. *Cards on the Table*
8. *A Caribbean Mystery*
9. *A Holiday for Murder*
10. *By the Pricking of My Thumbs*
11. *Poirot Loses a Client*
12. *The Mirror Crack'd*
13. *The Patriotic Murders*
14. *N or M?*
15. *The Moving Finger*
16. *Murder in Retrospect*
17. *A Pocket Full of Rye*
18. *Endless Night*
19. *Cat Among the Pigeons*
20. *The Man in the Brown Suit*

## Quiz 10: Characters

1. Jason Rafiel—*Nemesis*
2. Norma Restarick—*Third Girl*
3. Anne Beddingfeld—*The Man in the Brown Suit*
4. James Bentley—*Mrs. McGinty's Dead*
5. Justice Wargrave—*Ten Little Indians*
6. Superintendent Battle—*The Secret of the Chimneys, The Seven Dials Mystery, Easy to Kill, Towards Zero,* and *Cards on the Table*

7. Lucy Eyelesbarrow—*What Mrs. McGillicuddy Saw!*
8. Lady Frances Derwent—*The Boomerang Clue*
9. Dr. Arthur Calgary—*Ordeal by Innocence*
10. Mr. Shaitana—*Cards on the Table*

# Quiz 11: *Murder on the Orient Express*

## Characters

1. Monsieur Bouc, Director of Compagnie Internationale des Wagons-lits
2. Michel, the Wagon Lit Conductor
3. Ratchett
4. Colonel Arbuthnot
5. Linda Arden
6. Princess Dragomiroff
7. Countess Andrenyi
8. The dressmaker Paul Poirot
9. Hector MacQueen
10. Countess Andreny

## Clues

1. Twenty-three minutes to one
2. Mrs. Hubbard's sponge bag
3. On top of Hildegarde Schmidt's suitcase
4. In Hercule Poirot's compartment
5. There were no tracks in the snow.
6. 12
7. Princess Dragomiroff
8. To make the time of death appear to have occurred earlier
9. The position of the wounds on the victim's body
10. " 'member little Daisy Armstrong"

## Circumstances

1. Number one
2. Istanbul-Calais coach
3. $20,000
4. Poirot did not like his face.
5. Yugoslavia
6. A snowdrift covered the tracks.
7. The Lindbergh kidnapping
8. To curl his moustache
9. Piquet
10. Belgrade

# Quiz 12: *Ten Little Indians*

## Characters

1. Mr. Blore
2. Emily Brent
3. Mr. and Mrs. Rogers
4. Isaac Morris
5. Fred Narracott
6. Hugo Hamilton
7. General Macarthur
8. Assistant Commissioner Sir Thomas Legge and Inspector Maine
9. Philip Lombard
10. The hanging judge

## Clues

1. "Ladies and gentleman! Silence, please! You are charged with the following indictments:..."
2. Anthony Marston
3. Justice Wargrave

4. General Macarthur
5. Dr. Armstrong
6. Philip Lombard
7. Lombard, Armstrong, and Blore
8. The shower curtain was wrapped around the shoulders of a murder victim.
9. The wool was used to make a wig for one of the murder victims.
10. By reading the nursery rhyme

## Circumstances

1. Indian Island off the Devon coast in England.
2. August 8
3. Sticklehaven
4. The island was in the shape of an Indian's head.
5. *Swan Song*
6. Skilled Women's Agency
7. Dalmain
8. Mr. Owen recorded his voice on a gramophone record that was played for the guests after dinner.
9. *Emma Jane*
10. A troop of Boy Scouts

# Quiz 13: *The Murder of Roger Ackroyd*

## Characters

1. Inspector Raglan
2. Flora Ackroyd
3. Sherlock Holmes and Dr. Watson
4. The motto of the mongoose family, "Go and find out," from Rudyard Kipling's *The Jungle Book*.
5. Major Blunt was a big game hunter.
6. Roger Ackroyd discovered that Mrs. Ferrars killed her first husband.

7. The person who murdered Roger Ackroyd
8. Captain Ralph Paton
9. Mrs. Cecil Ackroyd
10. Major Blunt

## Clues

1. Flora Ackroyd
2. To hide the dictaphone that was sitting on the desk
3. A scrap torn from a handkerchief and a goose quill
4. Mrs. Ackroyd did not tell Poirot that she was in Mr. Ackroyd's study looking for his will and a piece of silver displayed in the silver table.
5. Mr. Raymond did not tell Poirot that he was in debt.
6. A gold wedding ring engraved with "March 13 from R"
7. Parker blackmailed his former employer.
8. Miss Russell had an illegitimate son, Charles Kent. He was a cocaine addict.
9. Poirot said he went to Cranchester to see the dentist to have a tooth pulled.
10. Ralph Paton's

## Circumstances

1. Fernly Park
2. Mah Jong
3. King's Abbot
4. Three Boars
5. Larches
6. A hairdresser
7. At a mental hospital in Cranchester
8. Until the next morning
9. Blue
10. Dog and Whistle

## Quiz 14: *Crooked House*

### Characters

1. Chief Inspector Taverner of Scotland Yard
2. Sir Arthur Hayward was the Assistant Commissioner of Scotland Yard.
3. Brenda worked as a waitress.
4. Sophia wanted to know the identity of the murderer so Charles would trust her. .
5. Arthur Hayward
6. Mr. Gaitskill
7. Mr. Agrodopolous, proprietor of the Delphos restaurant
8. Brenda Leonides and Laurence Brown
9. Clemency Leonides was a scientist.
10. Magda Leonides

### Clues

1. Eye drops
2. Associated Catering was headed for bankruptcy.
3. Sophia Katherine Leonides—She had the right qualities: brains, judgment, courage, a fair and un-biased mind, and generosity.
4. In the attic behind a cistern
5. Edith de Haviland
6. In an old dog kennel outside the back door
7. The block of marble fell several times, denting the flour, before the murderer was able to position it correctly.
8. The murderer had to stand on the old chair in order to balance the block of marble on the top of the door.
9. To throw the investigator off track
10. Aristide Leonides

## Circumstances

1. Mario's
2. Aristide Leonides owned a chain of restaurants, a catering business, second-hand clothes trade shops, and cheap jewelry stores.
3. Gay Shamrock
4. Sophia worked as an administrator in the Foreign Office.
5. Barbados
6. Swinley Dean
7. Degas
8. Associated Catering
9. Flackspur Quarry
10. "There Was a Crooked House"

## Quiz 15: *Death on the Nile*

### Characters

1. Lord Charles Windlesham
2. Colonel Race
3. Lord Dawlish
4. Cornelia Robson
5. Rosalie Otterbourne and Tim Allerton; Cornelia Robson and Dr. Bessner
6. Rosalie Otterbourne's mother was an alcoholic.
7. Kleptomania
8. To protect Linnet from Andrew Pennington
9. Linnet Doyle
10. Joanna Southwood

### Clues

1. Her grandfather, when she visited him in South Carolina

2. A boulder pushed off a cliff at Abu Simbel
3. Someone put a sleeping draught in Poirot's wine.
4. Miss Van Schuyler's
5. The pearls were stolen.
6. When the maid, Louise Bourget, was murdered
7. Pennington needed to get Linnet's signature to certain financial documents in order to prevent her from finding out that he was swindling her.
8. Poirot's discovery that the bottle of pink nail polish contained red ink, put him on the right track.
9. Linnet threatened to expose Dr. Bessner as a fraud.
10. Linnet's father's business transactions brought Miss Bowers's family to financial ruin.

## Circumstances

1. Cataract
2. Racy sex novels
3. *Under the Fig Tree*
4. *Snow on the Desert's Face*
5. Small pearl-handled pistol
6. *Carmanic*
7. "Frankie and Johnny"
8. *Murder on the Orient Express*
9. Miss Van Schuyler's theft of the pearls
10. Money

## Quiz 16: *The Murder at the Vicarage*

### Characters

1. Inspector Slack kept interrupting the vicar and would not let the vicar tell him about the clocks being set ahead.
2. Miss Marple was observing a golden crested wren.
3. A ferret

4. Lettice Protheroe
5. The vicar
6. Raymond West
7. Dr. Haydock
8. Dennis, the vicar's nephew
9. Martha Price Ridley
10. Mary could not cook or clean properly in spite of her high opinion of her own housekeeping skills.

## Clues

1. Anne Protheroe did not carry a handbag and her dress clung tightly, making it impossible to conceal a gun.
2. The clock, note, and pistol
3. Between 6:20 and 6:30 P.M.
4. A gun with a silencer attached
5. Lawrence Redding's
6. A phony call about a sick parishioner
7. Lawrence Redding
8. Anne Protheroe
9. The wrong stone was used in landscaping.
10. Griselda and Lawrence Redding were lovers before she married the vicar.

## Circumstances

1. Redding was painting Colonel Protheroe's daughter, Lettice, while she was clad only in a bathing suit.
2. The case of Miss Wetherby's gill of pickled shrimps that disappeared
3. To get a pregnancy test
4. "Sorry I cannot wait any longer, but…"
5. Misappropriation of church funds
6. 25 years
7. To conceal the stolen silver

8. So the police would not recognize the woman in the portrait
9. To see her daughter
10. Colonel Melchett dialed the wrong number when calling Dr. Haydock. He called Miss Marple instead and alerted her to the emergency at Mr. Hawes's house before he realized his error.

## Quiz 17: *Ordeal by Innocence*

### Characters

1. Hayes Bentley Expedition
2. Geophysicist
3. Kirsten Lindstrom
4. Dr. Calgary was in the Antarctic.
5. Hester Argyle
6. Paralytic polio
7. Five
8. MacMaster
9. Children's charities
10. Dr. Calgary

### Clues

1. The Borden ax murders
2. Kirsten Lindstrom
3. The Book of Job; the phrase was "The calamity of the innocent."
4. New evidence—Cyril Green saw a bright red car around 7:00 P.M. near the Argyle house on the night of the murder.
5. Tina was protecting Micky.
6. Micky used to climb the magnolia tree, which grew near the house. He could have climbed from the tree

into the window, entered the house unnoticed, and committed the murder.

7. "The cup was empty...." and "The dove on the mast..."

8. Jacko needed money immediately, or else he would be arrested.

9. The murderer had a motive for pinning the crime on Jacko.

10. Micky was bitter because Rachel took him away from his mother.

## Circumstances

1. The original name was Viper's Point. The new name was Sunny's Point.

2. Rubicon

3. Eels

4. He saw a photograph and an article in an old newspaper he was using to pack specimens.

5. Leo and Gwenda suspected each other of the murder.

6. Rachel and Leo hit Mary with their car while driving in New York. They were visiting an adoption agency. Mary was living with an aunt and uncle who were alcoholics. She did not want to return to their home after she was released from the hospital, so the Argyles adopted her.

7. "Criminal Types in Shakespeare"

8. Bicycle Accesssories Ltd.

9. Philip wanted to play detective and catch the murderer.

10. The murderer slipped the knife into Micky's pocket after she stabbed Tina.

# Quiz 18: *At Bertram's Hotel*

## Characters

1. Wilhelm and Robert Hoffman
2. Mr. Humfries was thought to be Mr. Bertram.
3. Henry
4. Chief Inspector Fred Davy of Scotland Yard
5. Colonel Luscombe and Mr. Egerton
6. Canon Pennyfather
7. Bridget
8. Because of Bess Sedgwick's wild and dangerous life-style, she thought she would be a bad influence on her daughter.
9. Archdeacon Simmons
10. He was a race car driver.

## Clues

1. Miss Marple learned that a certain plane was scheduled to leave for Lucerne at 9:40 A.M. She also realized that Bess was angry that Ladislaus showed up at the hotel.
2. To steal items to pawn and finance her trip to Ireland
3. Two
4. Ladislaus Malinowski's
5. Doppelganger
6. FAN 2266
7. To discover the identity of her father
8. She was afraid he would expose the fact that they had been lovers.
9. A mail train was robbed.
10. Inspector Davy suspected that the brains behind a notorious robbery syndicate was running the operation from the hotel.

## Circumstances

1. 1955
2. Around 1840, but no one knows for sure
3. Muffins
4. Miss Marple's uncle and aunt brought her to Bertram's when she was fourteen years old.
5. 3925
6. *Let Down Your Hair, Girls*
7. A television room
8. *Walls of Jericho*
9. Many believe it was Brown's Hotel, but Christie's biographer, Janet Morgan, believes it was Fleming's Hotel.
10. West End

# Quiz 19: *The Body in the Library*

## Characters

1. Mary, Colonel Bantry's maid
2. Colonel Melchett, Inspector Slack, and Superintendent Harper
3. He was a set decorator for Lenville Studios.
4. Rosy Legge
5. George Bartlett
6. Florence Small
7. Majestic
8. Conway Jefferson's legs were amputated as a result of an airplane crash.
9. Dinah Lee and Basil Blake; Mark Gaskell and Josie Turner
10. David

## Clues

1. Conway Jefferson wanted to adopt Ruby Keene.
2. Addie Johnson
3. Ruby Keene's fingernails were short and bitten. Miss Marple suspected that Ruby Keene was the type of girl to have long, polished fingernails.
4. Josephine Turner
5. A hearth rug
6. If Ruby Keene was to meet a boyfriend, why would she change into a shabby, old dress?
7. Basil Blake's
8. Mark Gaskell described Ruby's teeth as protruding back "...down her throat." However, Miss Marple noticed that the victim's teeth stuck out, not back.
9. Pamela Reeves believed she was preparing for a screen test.
10. Miss Marple set a trap that forced the killer to try and kill again.

## Circumstances

1. Minoan Fourteen
2. Venn's Quarry
3. *The Clue of the Broken Match*
4. Palais de Danse; Mr. Findeison
5. Scotland Yard
6. Basil Bake was laid up in a plaster cast after an injury received while rescuing four children and a dog from a burning building. With nothing to do but reflect, Basil became interested in designing.
7. Josie slipped while she was bathing and twisted her ankle.
8. Tango
9. Bridge
10. September

## Quiz 20: *Towards Zero*

### Characters

1. Mr. Treves
2. Andrew MacWhirter lost his job because he would not lie for his boss. MacWhirter could not find work and began drinking. His wife eventually left him.
3. Tennis
4. Thomas Royde
5. Old Bouncer, the family dog, had a sore paw and bit Audrey when she tried to play with him.
6. Superintendent Battle's nephew, Inspector James Leach
7. A heart condition
8. Will and George Barnes
9. Mary Aldin
10. Andrew MacWhirter

### Clues

1. Don smelled of a foul odor he received from rolling over a dead fish. MacWhirter noticed the same smell on someone's suit.
2. When the murderer brought his suit in to be dry-cleaned, he gave a false name, MacWhirter, one he took at random from the guest register at the hotel. When the real MacWhirter went to pick up his own suit, he was given the murderer's suit instead.
3. Nevile Strange
4. Mr. Treves's story was about the murderer, whom he knew as a child.
5. One of Nevile's little fingers was extraordinarily short.
6. To cause Mr. Treves to take the stairs, thus bringing on a heart attack

7. A man climbing a rope up the side of Lady Tressilian's mansion

8. The murderer used it to reach the bell wires and ring them. This caused the nurse to step out into the hall and see him, thus giving the murderer an alibi.

9. 1:30 A.M.

10. MacWhirter came looking for evidence to prove his theory. He saw a rope dangling From Lady Tressilian's window on the night she was murdered. It was raining and the rope should have been wet.

## Circumstances

1. September
2. Easterhead Bay
3. Malaya
4. The weather
5. Balmoral Court
6. "Think of the most difficult thing you can, and then set about doing it."
7. Chile
8. The superintendent pushed Ted Latimer out of the boat.
9. Nevile asked Kay for a divorce so he could remarry Audrey.
10. Audrey was really "paralyzed with fear" of being murdered.

## Quiz 21: Too Close for Comfort

1. b. Stifling, a large fire in the grate and the windows closed.
2. d. She will vicariously enjoy gardening by following Edwards around to see that he prunes properly.

3. a. A black jacket, stripped pants, bow tie, and patent leather boots.
4. b. Don a disguise, invent an assumed name, and devise her own plan.
5. c. Square armchairs, rectangular ornaments, horizontal and vertical lines, no curves, and books arranged according to height.
6. a. Stay calm and develop a plan of action.
7. c. Superintendent Battle never gives up. His fatherly manner and stoic patience caused you to confess. He convinced you that you would feel better if you came clean.
8. b. Listen closely to what the neighbors have to say. They know more than they realize.
9. d. "I can't give speeches. I get nervous and will probably stammer and look silly. I hate looking silly."
10. b. A soft poached egg, fresh rolls, and tea.
11. c. The latest fashions in women's clothing.
12. d. Arranging an innocent romance for you to ignite the lost passion.

# Quiz 22: Hercule Poirot, Detective Extraordinaire

1. Little gray cells
2. He considered himself the greatest mind in Europe.
3. His moustache
4. The police force
5. Belgian
6. Roman Catholic
7. Captain Hastings
8. Georges
9. Miss Felicity Lemon
10. Crème de Menthe

11. Papa Poirot
12. Green
13. 5 feet, 4 inches
14. Tonic
15. Air and ocean travel

## Quiz 23: Miss Jane Marple

1. Understanding human nature
2. Village parallels
3. St. Mary Mead
4. Miss Marple was an early riser. She started her day around 7:00 A.M.
5. 3 5
6. Clara
7. Raymond West
8. David West
9. China blue
10. White

## Quiz 24: Tommy and Tuppence Beresford

1. 1923
2. Tommy and Tuppence worked for the government in Intelligence.
3. Blunt's Brilliant Detectives
4. Albert
5. Cowley
6. Deborah and Derek
7. Andrew, Janet, and Rosalie
8. Mr. Carter
9. Hollowquay
10. A Black and Tan Manchester terrier named Hannibal

# Quiz 25: Mrs. Ariadne Oliver and Mr. Parker Pyne

1. Detective stories
2. Sven Hjerson
3. Apples
4. Thick, gray, and rebellious
5. Intuition and instinct
6. Smoking and drinking
7. 17 Richmond Street
8. Mr. Pyne worked for the government as a statistician.
9. 35 years
10. Mr. Pyne had a sliding pay scale.

## Quiz 26: Mr. Satterthwaite and Mr. Quin

1. 62–69 years
2. Masters
3. Mr. Satterthwaite left for the Riviera on the second Sunday in January and stayed until April.
4. Joining shooting parties in the country
5. Amateur photography
6. Mr. Satterthwaite proposed to a young lady in Kew Gardens.
7. Mr. Satterthwaite's main role in life was to listen to others.
8. *Homes of My Friends*
9. In London
10. Harley
11. Mr. Quin's motley-colored clothes were usually due to an illusion created by the light.
12. Dancer

## Quiz 27: Life in the Shadows

1. Arthur
2. Judith Hastings
3. Argentina
4. Mr. Parker Pyne
5. Poirot and Miss Lemon both had a passion for order.
6. Raymond West was a writer.
7. Mrs. West was an artist.
8. Joan Lempriere West
9. Sylvia
10. James Leach

## Quiz 28: Character Déjà Vu

1. f.    Violetta in *La Traviata*
2. i.    Maggie Moran in *Breathing Lessons*
3. a.    Scarlett O'Hara in *Gone With the Wind*
4. b.    Iago in *Othello*
5. g.    Anjuli in *The Far Pavilions*
6. d.    Marquise de Merteuil in *Dangerous Liaisons*
7. c.    Prince Charming
8. h.    Sleeping Beauty
9. j.    Daisy Buchanan in *The Great Gatsby*
10. e.    Cho-Cho-San in *Madama Butterfly*

## Quiz 29: Confidants and Accomplices

1. g.    Dame Laura Whitstable
2. j.    Mr. Baldock
3. e.    Llewellyn Knox
4. f.    J. Larraby
5. i.    Jane Harding
6. b.    Nina Anstey

7. d. Sidney Bent
8. h. Gerry Lloyd
9. c. "Sasha," Princess Hohenbach Salm
10. a. Hugh Norreys

## Quiz 30: Struggle for Survival

1. i. Denial of reality and need to control family
2. g. Obsessive love for a woman
3. c. Need to protect Milly Burt and destroy Isabella Charteris
4. f. Need to be safe and financially secure
5. d. Need to make lifelong amends to her sister
6. j. Wanting her daughter's happiness over her own
7. b. Blind love for Vernon Deyre
8. a. Repetitive pattern of involvement in abusive relationships
9. h. Need to support the underdog
10. e. Assumed her life would be like her parents'

## Quiz 31: *Giant's Bread*

1. c. Abbot's Puissant
2. c. A grand piano
3. a. To have enough money to marry
4. b. Nell did volunteer work at a military hospital.
5. a. Sebastian Levine
6. d. *The Prince of the Tower*
7. c. Vernon was hit by a car.
8. a. Vernon assumed she was pregnant.
9. d. Corporal George Green, a deserter
10. c. Emotional ties with everyone in his life

## Quiz 32: *Unfinished Portrait*

1. b.  Ten
2. a.  Celia was taught by her lady's maid.
3. c.  Math
4. a.  France
5. d.  Marguerite from *Faust*
6. c.  Judy
7. d.  *The Lonely Harbour*
8. a.  Celia's mother died.
9. c.  Dermont fell in love with another woman.
10. b.  Good storytelling

## Quiz 33: *Absent in Spring*

1. b.  Joan was going to visit her ill daughter, who was living in the Middle East.
2. a.  Their meeting was the catalyst that caused Joan to reflect on her life.
3. d.  Lizards popping out from everywhere
4. b.  Do not accept things at face value just because it is the easiest way to live life.
5. d.  Joan recited poetry to herself.
6. a.  Joan was very controlling and in denial of her family's problems.
7. c.  Little jumping Joan
8. b.  Averil was anxious to see her mother, because she noticed a change in Joan.
9. c.  Joan's good intentions faded as soon as she arrived home.
10. c.  A Shakespearean sonnet

## Quiz 34: *The Rose and the Yew Tree*

1. d.  St. Loo
2. c.  Hugh was hit by a drunk driver.
3. d.  He was a schoolmaster.
4. b.  His sister
5. d.  The Conservatives Party
6. c.  John jumped into the harbor to save a drowning child even though he could not swim.
7. b.  He wanted a cushy job.
8. b.  John took pity on her because of her abusive husband.
9. d.  Lady Tressilian
10. c.  Isabella's unselfish love

## Quiz 35: *A Daughter's a Daughter*

1. d.  Switzerland
2. b.  By spending a month alone in the middle of the desert
3. h.  "How to Be Alive Today"
4. c.  To South Africa to grow oranges
5. b.  To insist that Sarah move out and find a place of her own
6. c.  Three
7. d.  Sarah was addicted to cocaine, and her husband provided the finances for her habit.
8. a.  Gerry Lloyd, an old boyfriend
9. c.  Ann traded her quiet life for the party life.
10. b.  She knew Sarah would be unhappy and wanted revenge because Sarah had ruined Ann's life with Richard.

## Quiz 36: *The Burden*

1. a.   Mr. Baldock took pity on Laura and invited her for tea.
2. c.   Mr. Baldock was a history professor.
3. a.   Laura saved Shirley's life when the house caught on fire.
4. d.   To live on an island in a white house with green shutters and do nothing all day
5. b.   Medicine
6. c.   An owlish-looking man sitting at a gigantic desk, a sanitarium surrounded by pine trees, and the face of a suffering woman
7. d.   Camping alone in the desert
8. b.   Shirley realized she loved her first husband.
9. a.   Fatal Apple
10. c.   That Shirley paid for Laura's sin and canceled the debt between them

## Quiz 37: *The Adventure of Christmas Pudding and a Selection of Entrees* and *Double Sin and Other Stories*

1. c.   "DON'T EAT NONE OF THE PLUM PUDDING. ONE AS WISHES YOU WELL."
2. d.   The body of Mr. Clayton
3. b.   Lily Margrave, Lady Astwell's paid companion
4. c.   The letter from Mr. Farley requesting his advice
5. d.   "If you want to know the time, ask a policeman."
6. b.   Her luggage containing expensive miniatures was taken.
7. a.   To prevent a murder
8. a.   "The Adventure of Christmas Pudding"
9. a.   The doll wanted to be loved.
10. d.   To recover his stolen jewelry collection

11. b.  The ordeal was becoming physically draining.
12. c.  A dying man

## Quiz 38: *Dead Man's Mirror* or *Murder in the Mews*

1. "The Incredible Thief"
2. "Dead Man's Mirror"
3. "Triangle at Rhodes"
4. "Dead Man's Mirror"
5. "Murder in the Mews"
6. "Dead Man's Mirror"
7. "Dead Man's Mirror"
8. "Murder in the Mews"
9. "Triangle at Rhodes"
10. "The Incredible Thief"

## Quiz 39: *The Golden Ball and Other Stories* and *The Listerdale Mystery*

1. b.  A grand duchess trying to escape a forced marriage
2. c.  A small two-seater sports car
3. d.  An impersonator of a grand duchess who was fearful of being kidnapped
4. c.  An imitation stone necklace
5. d.  That he could behave courageously in an emergency
6. b.  The trousers James wore were not his.
7. b.  *Tosca*
8. a.  Her husband's company was headed for financial ruin and she could not abandon him during this ordeal.
9. d.  Terry was a gift from her brother.

10. a. An unknown benefactor paid the rent and upkeep.
11. b. Alix suspected her husband of being an escaped wife-killer.
12. c. Magdalen and Sir Edward had a romantic interlude ten years before and, upon separation, he pledged his eternal service.
13. a. He suspected her of killing her previous husband.
14. c. *Murder Most Foul*
15. b. Buying a sports car inspired "The Manhood of Edward Robinson"

## Quiz 40: *The Hound of Death and Other Stories*

1. c. Did a Belgian nun have supernatural powers or was it just spontaneous human combustion?
2. l. Strong signals warned the protagonist of imminent danger.
3. g. Was this a case of multiple personalities or a masterful plan of revenge?
4. j. Dickie Lawes's childhood nightmares became reality and were occurring in his adult life.
5. b. Mr. Lancaster was not afraid to move into a haunted house. This made the lonely ghost very happy.
6. i. Was Mrs. Harter receiving messages from her dead husband telling her to be ready for his arrival to take her to the other side, or was she being rushed to the grave by an earthly power?
7. d. The law said that a woman cannot testify against her husband, but what if she wanted to?
8. a. Distress calls from on the golf course led Jack to believe that his mind was playing tricks on him. He was tricked, but not by his mind.

9. f. A young heir came into his title and estate, but a greedy stepmother's supernatural powers left him behaving like a feline.

10. k. Silas Hamer was willing to pay any price for peace of mind.

11. e. Motherly love was too great a power for the medium, Simone. Her contact with the other world became her last.

12. h. A motorist, stranded on the Wiltshire Downs, took refuge in a nice family's cozy home. Once inside, he began receiving distress signals; the skeletons would not stay in the closet.

## Quiz 41: *The Labors of Hercules*

1. g. Poirot was assigned to locate a kidnapped Pekingese.

2. d. Poirot was hired to find the source of a multi-headed monster of gossip and rumor.

3. b. Poirot was trying to locate a graceful, doelike dancer who had "hair like wings of gold."

4. j. Poirot captured an unsavory, vicious gambling lord.

5. e. Poirot was in charge of cleaning up a political scandal about to be revealed by a seedy tabloid.

6. h. Poirot captured two raptor-like women who preyed upon innocent victims by blackmail.

7. k. Poirot saved a muscular, godlike young man from destruction.

8. f. Poirot busted a cocaine ring that was exploiting young girls.

9. a. Poirot was assigned to find and return a stolen painting depicting characters of "rich, voluptuous flesh."

10. l.    Poirot freed a group of wealthy widows under the influence of a greedy evangelist.

11. c.    Poirot was tracing a Renaissance goblet that had been stolen. His intention was not to return it to the owner, but to the nuns to whom it had been entrusted.

12. i.    Poirot lured a vicious guard dog out of a cellar nightclub named Hell.


## Quiz 42: *The Mysterious Mr. Quin*

1. b.    Mr. Quin's car broke down near the estate.
2. c.    "The blood spot on Mrs. Scott's ear"
3. a.    A man of magic
4. d.    Arlecchino
5. b.    Mr. Quin suggested a "Hedges and Highways" party.
6. d.    To build a house, plant a tree, and have a son
7. a.    "Give back what is not yours. Give back what you have stolen."
8. c.    Resonance, a high-pitched note that can shatter glass
9. b.    Mr. Quin
10. d.    *N or M?*
11. a.    The Duchess of Leith
12. b.    A rubbish heap


## Quiz 43: *Mr. Parker Pyne, Detective*

### Part One

1. b.    Mrs. Packington could not sit by and watch her husband waltz out of her life. At Mr. Pyne's advice, she changed her focus and filled up her own dance card.

2. e.   Mr. Parker Pyne killed two birds with one stone by sending two discontented clients on a wild-goose chase.

3. f.   Trust is a two-way street and 87 percent of the time dishonesty does not pay. Luckily, Mr. Parker Pyne was not born yesterday. He was able to turn the tables on a greedy young client.

4. a.   Mr. Wade had six months to win back his wife. Was Mr. Pyne successful, or did he have another problem to solve?

5. d.   The suburban family life was too comfortable for Mr. Roberts, so he paid a visit to Mr. Parker Pyne. For a mere five pounds, Mr. Pyne sent his client on a cloak-and-dagger mission.

6. c.   Mrs. Rymer strayed too far from her roots, but found happiness cutting cabbages in Cornwall.

## Part Two

1. b.   Blackmail led a husband to steal. Mr. Parker Pyne convinced the young man to go straight to his wife and confess the truth, but not the whole truth. After all, wouldn't a wife prefer a Don Juan for a husband over a fool?

2. d.   Mr. Parker Pyne was visiting the site near Damascus where St. Paul was lowered out of a window. This site was now a setting for masterful deception, but Mr. Parker Pyne was too smart for the criminal.

3. e.   A long way from home, Mr. Parker Pyne visited the rock of Behistun. But even on this sojourn he brought along a clipping from the newspaper that included his famous ad. This was his ticket to righting a wrong and freeing an innocent actress.

4. a.   Did history repeat itself? Two thousand years ago, racketeers robbed travelers and stored their booty

in Petra. This historic setting lent itself to thievery once again.

5. c.  He wanted the money *and* the girl. Murder was not too high a price to pay. This story took place on the *S.S. Fayoum* as it floated past the temples of Karnak.

6. f.  Mr. Parker Pyne was determined to continue his Greek holiday unrecognized. His plan was more than successful when the villain donned an all-too-familiar disguise.

## Quiz 44: *Partners in Crime*

1. e.  Francis and Desmond Okewood
2. d.  McCarty and Riordan
3. g.  Sherlock Holmes
4. b.  Thornley Colton, the blind detective
5. h.  Edgar Wallace
6. f.  Miss Polly Burton
7. a.  Hanaud
8. j.  Roger Sheringham
9. i.  Dr. Fortune and Superintendent Bell
10. c.  Inspector French

## Quiz 45: *Poirot Investigates*

1. e.  "The Million-Dollar Bond Robbery"
2. h.  "The Kidnapped Prime Minister"
3. n.  "The Chocolate Box"
4. j.  "The Adventure of the Italian Nobleman"
5. a.  "The Adventure of 'The Western Star'"
6. f.  "The Adventure of the Egyptian Tomb"
7. l.  "The Veiled Lady"
8. b.  "The Tragedy at Marsdon Manor"

9.  i.  "The Disappearance of Mr. Davenheim"
10. d.  "The Mystery of Hunter's Lodge"
11. k.  "The Case of the Missing Will"
12. g.  "The Jewel Robbery at the Grand Metropolitan"
13. m.  "The Lost Mine"
14. c.  "The Adventure of the Cheap Flat"

## Quiz 46: *The Regatta Mystery and Other Stories*

1. Morning Star
2. Mr. Parker Pyne
3. Women should always tell the truth to their confessor, their hairdresser, and their private detective.
4. An oyster shell border in the garden
5. Majorca
6. *Remembered Death*
7. The murderer dropped her g's.
8. Twenty-eight minutes past three
9. Sylvia turned to her brother, Alan.
10. On a cruise of the Nile River in Egypt

## Quiz 47: *The Tuesday Club Murders*

1.  h.  Old Mr. Hargraves
2.  c.  An unconscious man
3.  k.  Gardeners
4.  m.  Mrs. Green
5.  f.  Tommy Symonds, a naughty little boy
6.  i.  Farmers in Grey Wethers
7.  d.  A district nurse
8.  l.  Mrs. Trout
9.  a.  Poor Annie Poultny
10. g.  Walter Hones
11. e.  Mr. Badger, the chemist

12. j.  Mrs. Pebmarsh
13. b.  Mr. Peasegood, the vegetable peddler

## Quiz 48: *The Under Dog and Other Stories*

1. c.  His valet, George
2. b.  Word association
3. d.  *The Mystery of the Blue Train*
4. a.  "Murder in the Mews"
5. d.  The firstborn son will not live to inherit.
6. b.  "The Adventure of Clapham Cook" and "The King of Clubs"
7. a.  "The Submarine Plans"
8. c.  Mr. Quin
9. b.  "The Cornish Mystery"
10. c.  "The Market Basing Mystery"

## Quiz 49: *Three Blind Mice and Other Stories*

1. c.  As a radio play
2. d.  Queen Mary, mother of King George VI
3. b.  Miss Marple's Uncle Henry
4. c.  Miss Emily's refusal to see a doctor even though she was a hypochondriac
5. d.  The disappearance of the vicar's housekeeper
6. a.  Miss Marple's two cousins, Antony and Gordon
7. c.  Hercule Poirot
8. c.  Poirot located the Waverlys' kidnapped son.
9. d.  The victim's white, well-brushed teeth
10. a.  *The Murder at the Vicarage*

## Quiz 50: Stage Craft

1. Ambassadors Theater
2. *The Hollow*
3. *Black Coffee*
4. *Spider's Web*
5. *Alibi*
6. *The Patient*
7. *The Hollow*
8. *The Mousetrap*
9. *Ten Little Indians*
10. *Fiddlers Three*
11. *The Rule of Three*
12. *Witness for the Prosecution*
13. *Verdict*
14. *Akhnaton*
15. *Spider's Web*
16. *The Unexpected Guest*
17. *The Murder at the Vicarage*
18. *Hidden Horizons*
19. *Ten Little Indians*
20. *Fiddlers Five*

## Quiz 51: Play Adapations

1. e.  *Hidden Horizon*
2. c.  *Go Back for Murder*
3. a.  *Alibi*
4. b.  *Love From a Stranger*
5. d.  *Akhnaton*

## Quiz 52: *The Mousetrap*

1. d. "He is foreign and dark and elderly with a flamboyant moustache."
2. i. "She is a tall, pretty young woman with an ingenuous air, in her twenties."
3. g. "...is a middle-aged, square-shouldered man, very military in manner and bearing."
4. h. "She is a young woman of a manly type and carries a case."
5. a. "Medium height, wearing darkish overcoat, lightish scarf, and soft felt hat."
6. j. "The murdered woman served a prison sentence for causing the death of a child due to neglect."
7. b. "...is a cheerful, commonplace young man with a slight cockney accent."
8. e. "She is a large, imposing woman in a very bad temper."
9. f. "He is a rather arrogant but attractive young man in his twenties."
10. c. "He is a rather wild-looking neurotic young man."

## Quiz 53: *Verdict*

1. False—Anya was bitter because they were in exile from their home country.
2. False—Professor Hendryk felt that Lester had potential and had "the real stuff of which scholars are made."
3. False—Sir William offered Professor Hendryk an opportunity to have his wife treated with a new miracle drug that could cure her sclerosis.
4. True
5. True

6. False—Helen was killed in a traffic accident.
7. True
8. False—Hendryk was furious, but he was in love with Lisa Koletzky.
9. False—The play was booed by the audience on opening night.
10. True

## Quiz 54: *Black Coffee*

1. False—Sir Claud forced his son, Richard, to leave the army and move back home.
2. True
3. False—Sir Claud gathered everyone in his study and turned out the lights to give the thief a chance to return the formula anonymously.
4. True
5. True
6. False—Selma Goetz was Lucia's mother.
7. True
8. False—Inspector Japp investigated the murder.
9. True
10. False—Agatha was in Mesopotamia.

## Quiz 55: *Spider's Web*

1. False—Clarissa fooled both men by filling each of the three glasses from the same decanter.
2. False—Oliver Costello went to Copplestone Court to retrieve an incriminating slip of paper that had his name on it.
3. True
4. True

5. True
6. True
7. False—Miss Peake hid the body the second time.
8. True
9. False—Margaret Lockwood suggested that the play be a comedy.
10. False—The play ran for over two years.


## Quiz 56: *The Unexpected Guest*

1. True
2. True
3. False—Three people confessed to the murder and it may be inferred that a fourth person also confessed.
4. False—Richard Warwick drank because of his paralysis.
5. True
6. False—Henry Angell threatened to blackmail Julian Farrar.
7. False—Julian Farrar admitted to being in the study on the night of the murder.
8. True
9. False—Jan Warwick accidentally shot himself.
10. False—*The Unexpected Guest* ran for 604 performances.


## Quiz 57: Behind the Scenes

1. b.   *Death on the Nile*
2. e.   The temperature usually soared to around 130 degrees.
3. a.   Albert Finney, in *Murder on the Orient Express*
4. c.   *The Godfather, Part II*

5. b.   *Ordeal by Innocence*
6. c.   Margaret Rutherford
7. a.   Bette Davis
8. e.   *Murder on the Orient Express*
9. d.   *The Alphabet Murders*
10. e.   Peter Ustinov
11. c.   Bette Davis
12. b.   Three
13. a.   *Adventure, Inc.*
14. d.   Charles Laughton
15. c.   *Witness for the Prosecution*
16. c.   Joan Hickson
17. e.   Orson Welles
18. a.   The real Orient Express cars
19. d.   *Murder on the Orient Express*
20. d.   *Murder She Said*
21. b.   *Murder at the Gallop*
22. e.   *Ten Little Indians*
23. a.   *Murder on the Orient Express*
24. a.   Ingrid Bergman
25. d.   *Ordeal by Innocence*

## Quiz 58: Casting Calls

1. t.    Austin Trevor
2. m.    Basil Rathbone
3. ww.   Ann Harding
4. r.    Barry Fitzgerald
5. ee.   Ronald Reagan
6. o.    Cloris Leachman
7. jj.   Jessica Tandy
8. kk.   Gracie Fields
9. ll.   Roger Moore

10. x.  Tyrone Power
11. aa.  Marlene Dietrich
12. u.  Charles Laughton
13. nn.  Lionel Jeffries
14. ss.  Margaret Rutherford
15. s.  Hugh O'Brian
16. k.  Fabian
17. n.  Tony Randall
18. q.  Hayley Mills
19. mm.  Jacqueline Bisset
20. i.  Albert Finney
21. e.  Sir Richard Attenborough
22. h.  Mia Farrow
23. p.  Bette Davis
24. rr.  Elizabeth Taylor
25. bb.  Rock Hudson
26. tt.  Angela Lansbury
27. y.  Geraldine Chaplin
28. dd.  Sir John Gielgud
29. ii.  Cheryl Campbell
30. xx.  Maggie Smith
31. uu.  James Mason
32. qq.  Roddy McDowall
33. f.  Beau Bridges
34. gg.  Diana Rigg
35. cc.  Deborah Kerr
36. oo.  Olivia de Havilland
37. z.  Bill Bixby
38. vv.  Helen Hayes
39. g.  Donald Sutherland
40. pp.  Faye Dunaway
41. j.  Christopher Plummer
42. l.  Jean Stapleton
43. w.  Jonathan Cecil
44. hh.  Joan Hickson

45. a.　Piper Laurie
46. ff.　Lauren Bacall
47. d.　Peter Ustinov
48. b.　Jenny Seagrove
49. v.　Stephanie Zimbalist
50. c.　David Suchet

## Quiz 59: *Agatha*, the Movie

1. Vanessa Redgrave
2. Timothy Dalton
3. Dustin Hoffman
4. First Artists
5. Kathleen Tynan
6. Michael Apted
7. Dustin Hoffman
8. Kathleen Tynan and Arthur Hopcraft
9. Agatha Christie, Ltd. claimed that the story was not factual and that it defamed Christie.
10. Phil Feldman

## Quiz 60: Agatha Mary Clarissa Miller's Life and Times

1. September 15, 1890
2. Truelove
3. The gunman
4. Her sister, when she told Agatha the Sherlock Holmes story, *The Blue Carbuncle.*
5. Frederick Alvah Miller and Clara Boehmer
6. A series of heart attacks.
7. Her father was a wealthy expatriate.
8. 1926

9. Miss Dryden's
10. Agatha took a ride in an aeroplane
11. Major Bolton Fletcher
12. Cairo, Egypt
13. Agatha met Archie at a dance at Chudleigh.
14. Agatha became a "first aider" at a hospital.
15. 1919
16. The Canary Islands
17. 1971
18. Charlotte Fisher
19. False: Agatha was inspired by her sister to write her first detective story.
20. True
21. False; Agatha's first agent was Hughes Massie.
22. False; the inspiration for Hercule Poirot came from the Belgian refugees living at the parish of Tor.
23. False; the romance novel was *Absent in Spring*
24. True
25. False; Agatha was inspired to write *Death on the Nile* after her visit to the Middle East with her second husband, Max.
26. False; Agatha found it difficult to base her characters on real people, and hardly ever did so.
27. December 4, 1926
28. Eleven days
29. In a hotal spa, the Harrogate
30. Mrs. Neele; it was the name of her husband's mistress.

## PUZZLE 1—MYSTERY TITLES & MORE

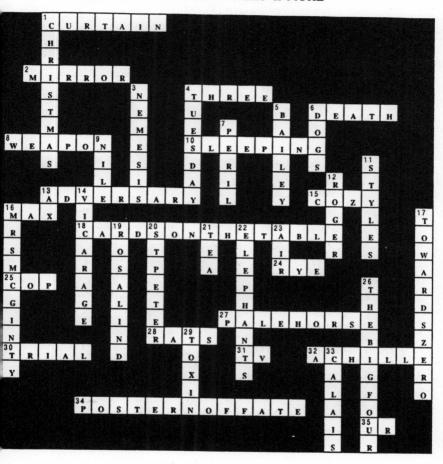

## PUZZLE 2—BRITISH TERMS

## PUZZLE 3—POISON & DRUGS

# Bibliography

Christie, Agatha. *The ABC Murders.* New York: Bantam Books, 1983.

_____. *Absent in Spring.* New York: Bantam Books, 1992.

_____. *An Autobiography.* New York: Bantam Books, 1977.

_____. *And Then There Were None.* New York: Bantam Books, 1983.

_____. *Appointment With Death.* New York: Berkley Books, 1984.

_____. *Black Coffee.* New York: Samuel French, Inc., 1961.

_____. *At Bertram's Hotel.* New York: Bantam Books, 1987.

_____. *The Big Four.* New York: Berkley Books, 1984.

_____. *The Body in the Library.* New York: Bantam Books, 1987.

_____. *The Burden.* Leicestershire: F.A. Thorpe (Publishing) Ltd., 1986.

_____. *By the Pricking of My Thumbs.* New York: Harper-Paperbacks, 1992.

_____. *Cards on the Table.* New York: Bantam Books, 1984.

_____. *A Caribbean Mystery.* New York: Bantam Books, 1987.

_____. *Cat Among the Pigeons.* New York: Pocket Books, 1959.

_____. *The Clocks.* New York: Bantam Books, 1988.

_____. *Come, Tell Me How You Live.* New York: Bantam Books, 1985.

_____. *Crooked House.* New York: Bantam Books, 1986.

_____. *Curtain.* New York: HarperPaperbacks, 1993.

_____. *A Daughter's a Daughter*. Leicestershire: F. A. Thorpe (Publishing) Ltd., 1978.

_____. *Dead Man's Folly*. New York: Pocket Books, 1961.

_____. *Dead Man's Mirror*. New York: Berkley Books, 1984.

_____. *Death Comes as the End*. New York: Bantam Books, 1984.

_____. *Death in the Air*. New York: Bantam Books, 1986.

_____. *Death on the Nile*. New York: Bantam Books, 1983.

_____. *Destination Unknown*. New York: HarperPaperbacks, 1992.

_____. *Double Sin and Other Stories*. New York: Berkley Books, 1984.

_____. *Dumb Witness*. New York: Berkley Books, 1984.

_____. *Easy to Kill*. New York: Pocket Books, 1967.

_____. *Elephants Can Remember*. New York: Berkley Books, 1984.

_____. *Endless Night*. New York: Bantam Books, 1985.

_____. *Evil Under the Sun*. New York: Dodd, Mead & Company, 1969.

_____. *Five Little Pigs*. New York: Berkley Books, 1984.

_____. *Funerals Are Fatal*. New York: Pocket Books, 1954.

_____. *Giant's Bread*. New York: Jove-Playboy/Berkley, 1990.

_____. *The Golden Ball and Other Stories*. New York: Bantam Books, 1987.

_____. *Hallowe'en Party*. New York: Berkley Books, 1991.

_____. *Hercule Poirot's Casebook*. New York: G. P. Putnam's Sons, 1984.

_____. *Hercule Poirot's Christmas*. New York: HarperPaperbacks, 1992.

_____. *Hercule Poirot's Early Cases*. Boston: G. K. Hall & Co., 1975.

_____. *Hickory, Dickory, Death*. New York: HarperPaperbacks, 1992.

_____. *The Hollow*. New York: G. P. Putnam's Sons, 1992.

_____. *The Hound of Death*. Leicestershire: F.A. Thorpe (Publishing) Ltd., 1968.

_____. *The Labours of Hercules*. New York: Berkley Books, 1984.

_____. *The Man in the Brown Suit*. New York: Berkley Books, 1984.

_____. *The Mirror Crack'd*. New York: Bantam Books, 1984.

_____. *Miss Marple: The Complete Short Stories*. New York: G. P. Putnam's Sons, 1985.

_____. *Mrs. McGinty's Dead*. New York: Bantam Books, 1987.

_____. *Mr. Parker Pyne, Detective*. Boston: G.K. Hall & Co., 1989.

_____. *The Mousetrap and Other Stories*. New York: Harper-Paperbacks, 1978.

_____. *The Moving Finger*. New York: Bantam Books, 1983.

_____. *The Murder at the Vicarage*. New York: Bantam Books, 1983.

_____. *Murder in Mesopotamia*. New York: Berkley Books, 1984.

_____. *Murder in the Mews*. New York: Berkley Books, 1984.

_____. *Murder in Three Acts*. New York: Bantam Books, 1988.

_____. *A Murder Is Announced*. New York: Bantam Books, 1986.

_____. *The Murder of Roger Ackroyd*. New York: Bantam Books, 1983.

_____. *Murder on the Links*. Leicestershire: F.A. Thorpe (Publishing) Ltd., 1977.

_____. *Murder on the Orient Express*. New York: Bantam Books, 1983.

_____. *Murder With Mirrors*. New York: Pocket Books, 1954.

_____. *The Mysterious Affair at Styles*. New York: Berkley Books, 1991.

_____. *The Mysterious Mr. Quin*. New York: Berkley Books, 1984.

_____. *The Mystery of the Blue Train*. New York: Bantam Books, 1987.

_____. *N or M?* New York: Bantam Books, 1988.

_____. *Nemesis*. New York: Pocket Books, 1973.

_____. *Ordeal by Innocence*. New York: Bantam Books, 1987.

_____. *The Pale Horse*. New York: HarperPaperbacks, 1992.

_____. *Partners in Crime*. New York: Bantam Blooks, 1983.

_____. *Passenger to Frankfurt*. New York: HarperPaperbacks, 1992.

_____. *The Patriotic Murders*. Boston: G. K. Hall & Co., 1990.

_____. *Peril at End House*. New York: Bantam Books, 1986.

_____. *A Pocket Full of Rye*. New York: Bantam Books, 1986.

_____. *Poirot Investigates*. New York: Bantam Books, 1985.

_____. *Postern of Fate*. New York: HarperPaperbacks, 1991.

_____. *The Regatta Mystery and Other Stories*. New York: Bantam Books, 1986.

_____. *The Rose and the Yew Tree*. Leicestershire: F. A. Thorpe (Publishing) Ltd., 1978.

_____. *Sad Cypress*. New York: Berkley Books, 1984.

_____. *The Secret Adversary*. New York: Berkley Books, 1991.

_____. *The Secret of Chimneys*. New York: Bantam Books, 1987.

_____. *The Seven Dials Mystery*. New York: HarperPaperbacks, 1991.

_____. *The Sittaford Mystery*. New York: Bantam Books, 1984.

————. *Sleeping Murder*. New York: HarperPaperbacks, 1992.

————. *Sparkling Cyanide*. Leicestershire: F. A. Thorpe, 1978.

————. *Spider's Web*. New York: Samuel French Ltd., 1956.

————. *Taken at the Flood*. New York: Bantam Books, 1987.

————. *They Came to Baghdad*. New York: Bantam Books, 1985.

————. *Third Girl*. New York: Bantam Books, 1987.

————. *Thirteen at Dinner*. Boston: G. K. Hall, 1989.

————. *Three Classic Mysteries Starring Miss Marple*. New York: Dodd, Mead & Company, 1977.

————. *The Tuesday Club Murders*. New York: Berkley Books, 1984.

————. *Towards Zero*. New York: Bantam Books, 1983.

————. *The Under Dog and Other Stories*. New York: Bantam Books., 1988.

————. *The Unexpected Guest*. New York: Samuel French Ltd., 1986.

————. *Unfinished Portrait*. New York: Arbor House, 1962.

————. *What Mrs. McGillicuddy Saw!* New York: Bantam Books, 1984.

————. *Why Didn't They Ask Evans?* New York: Bantam Books, 1984.

————. *Witness for the Prosecution and Other Stories*. New York: Berkley Books, 1984.


————. McAllister, Pam, and Dick Riley. *The New Bedside, Bathtub and Armchair Companion to Agatha Christie*. New York: Ungar, 1991.

————. Morgan, Janet. *Agatha Christie: A Biography*. New York: Alfred A. Knopf, 1985.

————. Sanders, Dennis, and Len Lovallo. *The Agatha Christie Companion*. New York: Berkley Books, 1989.